ANTIQUES IN THE HOME

A Golden Hands book

Marshall Cavendish, London

Edited by Gabrielle Weaver
Period Design by Katie Dyson
Guide to Antiques by Cooper-Bridgeman Library

Published by Marshall Cavendish Publications Limited
58 Old Compton Street
London, W1V 5PA

© Marshall Cavendish Limited 1972-73-74

This material first published by
Marshall Cavendish Limited in:
Golden Homes

This volume first printed 1974

Printed and Bound by Henri Proost, Turnhout, Belgium

ISBN 0 85685 061 6

This edition is not to be sold in the USA, Canada or the Philippines

Introduction

Your home reflects your personality and your taste, whenever it was built, whatever its style; with this book you can create the atmosphere of a period of your choice.

Perhaps you favour the balanced elegance of the Georgian period or the rich splendour of Tudor and Renaissance décor. If your choice is Art Nouveau for the bedroom or Victoriana for the lounge, this book shows you how to use fabrics and colours, bric-a-brac and objets d'art, as well as antique and reproduction furniture which mix and blend to suit both your taste and your budget!

Add to this a full colour guide to antiques, their value and their history, and you have a complete book for everyone who likes to create beautiful surroundings for themselves.

Contents

The Period Touch

An Introduction to Antiques and Price Guide

The period touch— Mediaeval living

The secret of a successful room scheme lies in knowing how to make the best of what there is. It may be an old chest, handed down through the family, a collection of cheap chairs from a local junk shop, or a few pieces of stark modern furniture. The important point is to learn how these furnishings can be used to advantage so they add personality to a room.

Today's home owners are lucky. Rooms do not have to be either totally antique or totally modern. In fact, the most successful ones often contain a selection of furniture from different periods, sympathetically arranged to give an individual touch.

This series traces the main developments and trends in interior design and furniture-making over the past centuries and tells you literally how to achieve the period touch by putting these ideas into action. Draw on the past for inspiration and you will be able to use a host of ideas to help in doing up your home.

Rare antique furniture is obviously too expensive for all except the lucky few who can afford it, but plenty of people do have perhaps one precious piece of old furniture that can often be used as the backbone of a room scheme. There is also a large range of often inexpensive reproduction furniture available in stores and furnishing shops in all parts of the world. Then there are junk shops and second-hand stores where you can browse among the jumble and find cheaper furniture that can be renovated.

The photographs in the series also help you 'get your eye in' so that you will be able to recognize a junk shop bargain and know it's something special when you see it. They also

Below. A period setting for the dining room, with a refectory table, benches and heavy chairs with carved backs. Also typical are the panelled walls and beamed ceiling.

give you ideas on how to use this type of furniture in your home.

Achieving the period touch does not necessarily mean that a whole room has to be crammed with antiques of one particular age to be successful. It means knowing how to give a room a period 'feel'.

The series shows how rooms have been planned through the ages and how to adapt the trends of long ago in a modern way. The photographs of rooms in new and famous old houses add extra inspiration.

With this increased knowledge you will be able to give more character to room schemes when planning a new home or re-vamping an existing room.

The first chapter in this series deals with life in Mediaeval times, and the interior design schemes of the 15th and 16th centuries. After establishing the major design aspects of this period, it goes on to give hints on ways of applying a period touch to the rooms in a modern house.

Mediaeval living

Built-in furniture is by no means a modern trend. In the 15th and 16th centuries furniture often depended on the walls for support. Huge four-poster beds would be built into oak-panelled rooms. The bed head and foot would be part of the walls. A tester was suspended from the ceiling and curtains hung from it so the bed could be totally enclosed at night to make almost a room within a room. The curtains, which kept out draughts, would be made from leather or thick tapestry.

The bed was often in the main room of the house. The dining table and stools or benches were mobile and would be put away when not in use, or could be carried round so meals could be served in different parts of the house.

Seating would be built in round the walls in the form of stone benches covered with carpets. Desks, too, were built in, relying on the walls for support at one end.

Comfortable padded upholstery had not been invented, so chairs were fairly spartan, often

with elaborately carved backs which echoed the Gothic architectural designs. There were X-shaped folding chairs with leather seats. Chairs always had arms until about the 1640's, when wide skirts were the fashion for women and stools were given high backs. Flat-topped chests were used as seats, or there were oak settles with high backs, benches and three-legged stools to sit on.

In simple kitchens there were chairs with rush seats. These are still being made in the attractive Mediaeval pattern and look lovely in a modern country pine kitchen. Basket work chairs were also used in simpler homes.

Possessions were stored in chests; it was not until the 17th century that chests of drawers began to take their place. There would be a court cupboard in the main room where the family plates would be displayed. This was usually a fairly heavy piece of oak furniture with four elaborately carved supports holding three 'table tops', one above the other.

Colour was of great importance in those days

and it is difficult now to realize how bright a Mediaeval room would have looked. The walls would be hung with vivid fabrics and tapestries, and brocade hangings in rich houses. Oak was the most popular wood. It would either be polished to a rich brown or it would be pale yellow. The woodwork and furniture would be carved, then gilded and painted.

Although furnishings were of necessity kept to a minimum, a Mediaeval room with its beamed ceiling would make up in colourful warm decorations for the draughtiness of the building. Carpets were not used on the floor, which was probably stone, and often covered with rush matting.

Achieving the period touch

There are several ways of giving rooms a period feeling. You don't have to turn a whole room into a Mediaeval banqueting hall, it can merely be a small corner which, by clever arrangement of furniture and accessories, has the right effect.

In the dining room

Use a refectory table and benches, then look for an old oak chest to put along the wall on one side of the room. Paint the walls white and hang a rug or a length of tapestry-effect fabric behind the chest. On either side of the rug hang a small collection of pewter or wooden plates as extra decoration. This will make an attractive period corner.

In the living room

The idea of built-in furniture and trestle tables that are easy to move when not in use is extremely practical these days, especially in small homes where there is eating and sitting in one room. For the table top, stain pine planks dark to look like rich oak, do the same with trestles, and this will make a practical mobile table.

For seating use stools or benches which can be pulled out into the middle of the room round the table when there are visitors. When you're not entertaining, the table can be stored away in a convenient place (like under the stairs), so you have the extra space the rest of the time and the room is not permanently crammed with furniture.

Panelled walls are more difficult to copy. However, in Britain, where many old public houses are being re-furbished, the old panelling is often removed and sold. If you are lucky enough to find some, you can use it attractively in your home. Junk emporia are another good source for this type of thing.

Make a wide ingle nook fireplace which takes up the whole of one end of the living room. Keep an eye open for an old beam to use across the top of the mantel. On either side of the fire build in small settles; these could be made of pine, again stained dark to look like oak.

Cover the floor with inexpensive squares of rush matting. Use the idea of rich colour by hanging rugs or large squares of bright fabric on the walls. It is possible to pick up beautiful old rugs cheaply at auction sales, where you can often also find large damask curtains from big houses. The fabric from these can be used as wall hangings. If the colours have softened too much but the fabric is still strong, which is often the case, it can be dyed to the colour of your choice.

Keep other furnishings simple, with perhaps two old oak stools that can be used as occasional tables. Then add your own comfortable chairs. Although the seating will not be Mediaeval, the room will have a definite feeling of that era. You could also add interesting ornaments in the form of old spears or arrow heads, or even antlers (bought from a junk shop). An old wooden candlestick would look effective on a big chest, where you could also keep a bowl of fruit.

In the bedroom

The idea of a built-in four-poster bed is well worth thinking about. Drapes were simple in Mediaeval days, so it would be quite easy to do. With modern central heating, the drapes would not need to be long enough to pull all the way round the bed.

For a bed head and foot, use two old panelled pub screens. Alternatively use large floor-to-ceiling sheets of blockboard which can then be covered with lengths of velvet, imitation tapestry or damask fabrics, even leather or a good imitation, which was a favourite in those days. These fabrics can be tacked to the blockboard underneath.

The tester can be a simple pelmet with a straight hem, tacked to a batten which is then fixed to the ceiling between the bed head and foot on each side. Hang curtain rails inside the pelmet and make the curtains in a fabric that

BRIAN MORRIS

BAVARIA—VERLAG

Far left. This house dates back to 1330, and was restored in the 1860s, hence the Gothic style windows with lattice panes.
Left top. This modern dining room has a Mediaeval feeling, with its whitewashed walls, long refectory table, rush seated chairs and converted church pews.
Left. An original old dining room in a German house. This is a period style dining room with a beamed ceiling, rough table with stripped wood door and a stone flag floor.

matches the rest of the bed. Finish the effect with a padded coverlet to match or a large sheep skin or goat skin thrown over the bed casually—expensive perhaps, but certainly effective.

Other furnishings in the bedroom should be kept to a minimum, with perhaps a chest at the foot of the bed and a carved armchair. Dressing table and clothes storage can all be built in to be unobtrusive.

In the kitchen

Have a refectory table for eating at one end of the kitchen. It is quite easy to make your own

---

Woods and colours of the era

Oak—*yellow and brown*	*Scarlet*
Ash	*Purple*
Sycamore	*Turquoise*
Maple	*Ultramarine*

---

from pine or elm which can be left in its original golden yellow colour or stained to a deep rich brown. Use rush-seated chairs round the table.

Modern built-in kitchen units can be given a period touch by the design of their door panels.

Above. *This large four-poster bed is hung with tapestry. Impressive, but it has competition from the weaponry on the wall and the rich panelling.*

Hang simple rustic cooking utensils from wrought iron circular holders near the stove—a highly practical storage idea. Collect wooden platters for the dresser; modern ones can be bought cheaply in kitchen shops. Earthenware cooking things would also look good in a kitchen of this type. A gate-leg eating table is also a good idea; these tables were introduced in the 1600s.

This chapter, the second in the series, moves on to the Tudor and Renaissance era, and into the 17th century. It covers the many different crafts popular at that time, and goes on to give ideas on how to recreate a Jacobean dining room in a modern house.

The Renaissance style that spread across Europe was a great contrast to the heavily ornamental style of the Gothic era. It began in Italy where the classical designs of Ancient Rome inspired art, architecture, and furniture design, and brought to Britain a flavour of refreshing simplicity and balance.

Interior design and architecture began to follow fashion, and at that time the trend-setter

The period touch— Tudor and Renaissance

was Italy. English craftsmen, however, had difficulty translating some of the classical Italian ideas, and furniture design was often muddled with the result that elaborately carved

Below. *An elegant library. Note the heavily carved furniture and panelling of the bookcases, the splendid stone fireplace, and the wrought iron firebasket and fireback.*

PICTUREPOINT

5

pieces merely looked clumsy. It took many years for the designs to settle down and translate themselves to English homes in a more shapely way.

The difference in designs for town and country homes began to be increasingly marked. Town furniture, for richer families, became more and more elaborate, while country furniture reverted to a rustic and functional simplicity little influenced by the dictates of fashion.

New wealth and accumulated possessions during the 16th and 17th centuries resulted in the invention of a whole range of storage furniture. For the first time chests of drawers appeared on the scene, as did cupboards with doors, and large 'press' cupboards used for storage in living rooms and halls; most were free-standing and some had secret hiding holes built into them. Books were stored in open bookshelves or in tall cases with glass-fronted doors.

The great hall was the centre of life in the larger English homes of the Tudor Age. There would be a high table for eating standing on a dais at one end of the hall.

Walls were often oak panelled and hung with rich materials, tapestries, or canvas painted to look like tapestry, or wall coverings made from gilded and embossed leather. Elaborate chimney pieces were an important room feature. Furniture, too, was large and imposing: upright chairs had wooden arms and padded backs, and seats that were covered in rich fabrics.

Beds were not built-in during the 16th century but they were among a family's most important and treasured possessions. Children slept on low truckle beds, and if they were in the same room as their parents the beds would be wheeled away neatly to be stored under the big four-poster during the day. The four-poster bed was something of a status symbol. They were very large, elaborately carved with strapwork, and some would have half-testers, or canopies, hung with rich materials.

During the 16th century refectory tables were installed, mainly in largish rooms. In smaller homes, which had 'dining parlours', tables were suited to the size of the room and could be enlarged to accommodate guests. Draw-leaf, drop-leaf, and gate-leg tables, usually with turned legs, were invented and soon became popular.

One space-saving idea was a chair-table: a big armed chair whose high back was on hinges so it could be swung over until it rested on the arms and formed a table top. Long wooden settles with high backs were designed in the same way—instant tables for a banquet.

In the late part of the century the back-stool was invented and began to appear in dining rooms. This was the original dining chair—normally with an upholstered seat and back rest but, to allow room for the fashionable farthingale skirts of the time, no arms.

Carpets became more numerous, although they were used on floors in only the most opulent of houses. In Stuart and Jacobean days the usual thing was for oriental carpets, mainly from Turkey, to be used for upholstery and cushion covers, or to cover tables and court cupboards. The colours were strong and bright, a mixture of red, white, blue and yellow forming

Top left. A modern kitchen/dining room with a period touch. Note the oak gate-leg table and antique chairs. The plain white ceiling with its inset spots and white floor do not detract from the period feeling.
Left. This dining hall is in a house that was built in 1634 and was formerly occupied by Kipling. Most of the decor, particularly the panelled walls, heavy furniture, and the crest on the chair backs, is authentic.

patterns of leaves and flowers.

Painted furniture lost favour as the Renaissance progressed into the 17th century. Instead, surfaces were left plain and finished with a high polish; carving and surface patterns were added in the form of elaborate inlays, marquetry or veneers. Baroque designs—then mainly opulent decorations of carved birds, fruit and flowers—were developed in Italy and spread across Europe.

Louis XIII of France made painted ceilings fashionable, and stucco decorations with wall niches in which to display sculptured figures. The walls were hung with colourful tapestries, woven in either Mortlake (London, England) or Brussels (Belgium), or decorated with paintings. Carpets were still used only on the floors of the richest houses, and floors elsewhere were mainly of marble, polished wood or Delft tiles.

But still the most important piece of furniture was the bed—a magnificent edifice of turned wood and lavish hangings whose tester would frequently be topped with ostrich plumes at each corner.

In the middle of the 17th century Louis XIV began his reign and the French style flourished. The art of marquetry was perfected and furniture was patterned with intricate floral designs which were influenced by the beautiful Dutch still-life paintings then in vogue. The Palace of Versailles in France became the ultimate showpiece of Baroque design which then spread to England and, after the Restoration, became the fashion.

Furniture of this period is now worth a fortune and is far out of reach of the ordinary person's pocket. However, a clever home craftsman can gain hours of pleasure from copying or adapting ideas for veneers, inlays, and marquetry from the lavish styles of the period.

Here is a brief guide to the different crafts:

Veneering

This is a way of making a decorative pattern on a solid piece of wood. Different types of wood are thinly sliced, arranged into patterns, and glued, then smoothed and polished so that the main effect is derived from the different grains. In the 17th century walnut veneers were popular but beautiful effects can be achieved with other types of wood.

Inlays and marquetry

Inlays of the Renaissance and the 17th century were made from hard stones like lapis lazuli and agate, or from ivory, mother-of-pearl and tortoiseshell. Marquetry is the use of differently coloured woods to achieve a decorative effect.

Both are done by cutting a quarter-inch strip from a cabinet front or table-top. The groove is

BRIAN MORRIS

THE NATIONAL TRUST/JOHN BETHELL

then filled with the coloured stones (inlays) or woods (marquetry). These can be arranged to produce complex and beautiful patterns; the surface is then smoothed and polished.

Great master of the art was a Frenchman called André Charles Boule, who lived from 1642 to 1732; the main materials he used were Tortoiseshell, pewter and brass. Boule could produce really stunning results with materials of such high quality.

Parquetry

This, like marquetry, is a form of wood mosaic that was also popular during the 17th century. Wood of many different colours was inlaid to form geometrical patterns that were smoothed to provide a beautiful surface finish.

Intarsia

Another form of marquetry, popular in the 17th century, in which the wood was positioned to make pictorial inlays.

Gesso

A form of gilt decoration, it became popular towards the end of the 17th century. A piece of furniture was carved to achieve the approximate desired shape then painted with several coats of Gesso mixture that was prepared from chalk and parchment-size. When dry, it was sanded down smoothly then gilded.

Lacquer and japanning

The second half of the 17th centruy saw the arrival of lacquered furniture from the Far East which sparked off a craze for furnishings in the Oriental style. Mirrors, chairs and cabinets were the most popular pieces—painted brightly in red, green, gold and black then lacquered to give them a shine.

Second half of the 17th century

Luxury became ornamental rather than plushly cushioned. Rooms were decorated with gilded plasterwork, and rich brocades were used for upholstery. In England, cotton quilts and hangings from India, which were richly patterned by a special method of painting and dyeing, became popular.

A suite of chairs became fashionable—couches, stools, upright chairs with wooden arms and plain upright chairs without arms, all upholstered in rich brocades or tapestries.

Woven canework was introduced from China and India, and became popular on chairs and couches with carved or, more often, turned legs. Gradually, English, French and Dutch furniture became less heavy and more elegant, and was decorated with brass, silver and bronze.

English rooms were often panelled then decorated with elaborately carved cornices along the tops of walls and above doors in a curved Baroque style. One of the most famous carvers was Grinling Gibbons, whose work,

usually in limewood, can still be found in some English houses.

The oak Jacobean style flourished during this time and lasted well into the 18th century, providing the inspiration for early American designs dating from the late 17th century.

Achieving the period touch

Small modern houses are not ideally suited to the heavily ornamented designs of Renaissance and Baroque: a huge stuccoed chimneypiece topped with gilt just wouldn't go into a smallish modern sitting room. So the art of lending a room the period touch is to be more sensitive and selective.

Just a small corner filled with one period piece selected with discrimination will set just the right tone, and the 'period piece' you choose could easily be one that is made at home using modern power equipment instead of the craftsman's tools. The designs of some beautiful old furniture are reasonably easy to copy—a craftsman's training and experience are not necessary.

A Jacobean oak stool, for example, would not be too difficult for an amateur to make on a home workbench, but would be prohibitively expensive to buy. These stools were made with a flat seat of plain design and moulded edges; the four sturdy legs were 'turned' in a simple design; plain 'stretchers', or strips of wood, joined the legs together at the bottom and under the seat to keep the stool firm. Photographs in this series will inspire ideas for other things to copy.

In the dining room

A Jacobean dining parlour is an attractive period idea that would be quite easy to recreate in a modern home. Reproduction Jacobean furniture is popular today and not difficult to find. Oak chairs with carved backs and turned legs would fill the bill, but a set of Jacobean stools set round a plain gate-leg or draw-leaf table which can be extended for guests would be simpler.

Latticed windows give the right Jacobean effect, but the furnishings and colours should help to complete the atmosphere. An oak chest will make a Jacobean-style serving table, or an ordinary table covered with a floor-length cloth of deep red, blue or green washable velvet; a glass top to protect the velvet is a practical idea.

Ornate picture frames discovered in junk shops for hanging reproduction prints of the famous Dutch Old Master paintings will add an attractive touch. Walls were usually panelled, with beamed ceilings, but in a modern house plain walls and ceilings are somehow more effective.

A Spanish dining room of the era would also be attractive to recreate, using a long oak table and high-backed chairs, the seats and backs of which can be covered in mock leather of rich blue or red. The upholstery can be attached with dome-headed brass tacks to produce a studded effect.

A final touch could be a fringe around the seat and under the upholstery on the back of each chair. A simple wrought-iron candelabra hung above the table adds a realistic touch. The floor could be plainly tiled, or laid with linoleum or lino tiles in a chequer-board pattern.

Woods and colours of the era	
Oak	Pine
Walnut	
Cypress	Crimson
Ebony	Emerald green
Chestnut	Gold

BAVARIA-VERLAG

The period touch— Tudor and Renaissance: 2

This chapter completes the theme of the Renaissance and the 17th century, with more ideas on how to achieve the period touch. It explains how to recreate a living room similar to the grand halls of the Renaissance era, and how to decorate a bedroom typical of the 17th century, with details of the styles which were popular in France and Spain at that time.

In the living room

Combined rooms for living, eating and sleeping were common in Renaissance days. An attractive idea for a long and fairly high living room—perhaps two rooms that have been knocked into one—would be to make a 'high table' for eating at one end of the room with seating at the other end. Part of the floor would have to be raised like a small stage, two or three feet from the ground with steps leading up to it. To get this effect you should construct a strong platform, at one end of your lounge. A basic knowledge of carpentry is all you will need to build this simple structure.

On the platform, place an oak refectory table and oak chairs with perhaps cane seats and backs. Good reproduction furniture of this type is readily available—the original would ob-

THE NATIONAL TRUST/JOHN BETHELL

THE NATIONAL TRUST/JOHN BETHELL

Above left. A 17th century look has been given to this modern living room, with its typical small-paned windows. The formal arrangement of furniture adds to the effect.
Above. The panelling and plasterwork of this house are typical of the Renaissance era. The furniture in this living room is mostly later, but the period feeling is retained.
Above right. The carved oak posts of this Henry VIII four-poster bed have the original colouring and gilding. The patchwork quilt is Victorian, and the tapestries are Flemish.

viously be too expensive. Alternatively, it would be possible to make a simply styled refectory table from elm. Use an oak chest as a serving table.

Comfortable seating can be arranged round

an open fireplace at the other end of the room. By covering modern easy chairs with tapestry-type fabrics, it is easy to keep the period feeling. Panelling was the usual wall covering, or walls were plain white with beams. The latter would be the easier to copy, with brass wall sconces to hold lights and a brass chandelier over the table.

Halls were often used as living rooms, particularly in Holland and Germany. Staircases were elaborately carved affairs without carpets on the treads. You can obtain a period effect by stripping, sanding and sealing your existing staircase.

It's often a good idea in a small house to knock out the wall between the hall and the living room, giving a much-needed feeling of increased space. This can then be transformed

into a 17th century style hall-living room.

A plain tapestry or leather-covered screen would have been used at the foot of the stairs to keep out draughts. Old screens are fairly easy to buy and inexpensive to renovate with a new covering of simulated leather, fixed with brass dome-headed nails.

There would have been a large carved oak cupboard for storing linen and perhaps an oak settle. So search round antique and junk shops for furniture of this type to get the right effect. Large cupboards like this are an excellent storage idea and old ones are among the best bargains in second-hand furniture shops because so many people have replaced them with modern fitted unit storage. However, in a sparsely furnished period style room, a large carved cupboard looks effective and its roomy

interior shelving adds vital storage space.

Choose cast iron or brass candelabra or wall sconces for lighting. Reproduction ones are inexpensive. Choose other accessories in the form of large pictures (use modern prints of old masters in elaborate frames), helmets, breast plates and armoury fixed on the walls as decoration.

These accessories are fun to collect from junk shops and would be enough to complete the period touch. All you then need to add are comfortable chairs. These could be modern ones, covered in leather, deep red velvet or a tapestry-type fabric, which would not detract from the period atmosphere of the room.

A French 17th century style living room would look attractive. In those days, the walls were hung with fabric; probably brocade in a floral pattern. Modern vinyl wallpapers are so cleverly designed that it is not difficult to find a good pattern that looks just like 17th century brocade. Gold is an ideal colour to choose, with white paintwork.

The floor in those days may well have been parquet, which you will find quite easy to lay for yourself with the minimum of know-how. Also there are some excellent DIY kits for the purpose on the market, which simplify the work enormously. Another alternative would be to sand and seal the existing floor.

Rugs would have been Persian or Turkish, and these are still being made in the same traditional style. It is also possible to buy good imitation ones made from cotton which cost less than half the price of the same thing. Alternatively, inexpensive large old Turkish or Persian rugs can sometimes be found in junk or second-hand furniture shops. Another idea would be to choose a fitted carpet with a period-style Persian pattern.

17th century seating was formal—well sprung easy chairs and sofas with deep upholstery as we know them today had not been invented. There would have been a suite of upright chairs and a couch, all with carved wooden legs and padded seats.

A modern living room needs to be comfortable even though it is decorated in period style, so the best way to achieve comfort as well as a period effect would be to cover existing easy chairs in a gold brocade fabric that ideally matches the wallpaper. Brocade is an expensive fabric, but there are excellent modern simulated brocades, often in a mixture of cotton and synthetic fibres. These are cheaper and look good when used carefully.

You can add to the 17th century feeling by placing two upright chairs against the wall at one end of the room, with perhaps a small chest, cabinet or writing table between them. Cover the chair seats in fabric to match the wallpaper or in tapestry.

Windows would have been covered with shutters and plain long curtains hung on a pole. Choose a gold-coloured fabric that matches the wallpaper or the upholstery.

An enormous ornate fireplace would be too

Left. A late 17th century atmosphere has been achieved in this modern living room, with its open fire and polished floor. The marquetry side table dates from the 1600s.

overpowering in today's smaller rooms. In England and North America, particularly, it is possible to buy excellent reproduction fireplaces, often made from glassfibre. These are scaled down in size to suit the smaller proportions of more modern houses. They come in a wide range of period styles and it should not be difficult to find one that is based on an actual Louis XIV design of the 17th century. Make the fireplace an open one with wrought iron fire dogs to decorate the grate.

Mantelpieces of the period were fairly small and not used too much for holding things, so don't crowd the mantelpiece with ornaments. Stick to the period style by arranging three or four Chinese vases on the mantelpiece. These vases were the most popular ornaments of the period, and are relatively cheap to buy from junk stalls or even in modern reproduction form from shops dealing in Oriental goods. Add floral decoration in the form of two orange trees standing on the floor in ornamental cache-pots.

Wall sconces holding candles were a fashionable form of lighting. Again there are excellent

MICHAEL DUNNE

Above. A splendid Portuguese travelling bed gives this modern bedroom the Spanish look popular in the 17th century. Furniture of later eras adds to the period effect.

reproduction lights of this type on the market, fitted with electric 'candle' bulbs. The originals would have been in silver or wood, carved and gilded. The reproduction ones are in imitation silver or gilt and look effective.

Large mirrors were popular in Louis XIV's day, when the art of using a mirror to give a room more light or space was perfected. These mirrors would frequently be hung in elaborate gilded frames between two windows. The least expensive way of getting the right effect is to buy a large old picture frame and put a mirror inside it.

Renovating the gilding is a simple job. First use a damp rag and an old toothbrush to remove surface dirt from the nooks and crannies of the frame. Wipe over with a rag soaked in turpentine substitute, then use a good gold paint to re-touch the frame. The best one, which is available in most parts of the world, is a gold paste which you smooth on with your index fingers.

This paint is the one most commonly used by antique restorers and picture framers.

A till mirror in a high rectangular frame is an excellent way of giving a room more height. Another French style was to set large mirrors into an alcove wall. The mirrors would often have curved tops. Underneath the mirror would be an upright settee with carved legs and arms and an upholstered seat and back.

Making an arrangement like this is an attractive way of adding space and could easily be copied. A full size mirror to cover the alcove wall would be far too expensive. Instead use large mirror tiles or four smaller mirrors, screwed to the wall to make one big one. Upright settees in the 17th century style can be found in junk shops and there are also good reproduction ones to be found in furniture stores. The settee could be upholstered in a gold fabric to match the rest of the room.

Tapestry cushions were popular accessories. These would be ideal to make, and a Louis XIV or 17th century pattern could be copied easily by someone who is keen on this craft. A good needlework shop will sell canvases with a pattern of the period already marked out and ready to be sewn. Period chair seat patterns for tapestry are also available from needlework shops. Tapestry fabrics are also available if you prefer to buy it in this form.

In the bedroom

The old idea of a low truckle bed that rolls away underneath a larger one during the daytime is one that can be up-dated usefully. Make truckle beds for the children—they can also be used when there are overnight guests. A low truckle bed could be made of a simple pine frame with boards running across it to support a foam mattress. It should be fixed on easy-move castors so that it can be wheeled away for storage under the parents' double bed.

When visitors are staying, the truckle beds are wheeled out for the children to sleep in, and the visitors then use the children's bedroom. This is a neat way of utilizing space in a small house. Having children sleeping in the main bedroom for the odd night is fun for them and means you have the bonus of extra bedroom space for visitors whom you may not otherwise be able to make room for.

There are some attractive ideas for getting the period touch in a more decorative way. For example, make a French 17th century style bedroom. In those days the bedroom would have been in an alcove off the main living room, but the decoration ideas are easily adapted to a present day bedroom. A popular colour scheme of the age was cornflower or French blue and white. This is an ideal colour to choose for a bedroom because it is attractive, yet restful.

Start with the bed—a four-poster with hangings. This would be expensive to buy, but could be made quite easily. Start by making the bed base about 2ft 6in. high, and fix round or turned posts to the four corners of the base to support the tester. Then make a frame on top to support the tester hangings. Stain the woodwork dark to look like polished oak, or paint it blue to match the fabric colour. Once again the construction of the bed itself is quite a simple task for the home handyman.

For the hangings, choose a plain cornflower or French blue fabric that looks like silk. Add pattern in the form of a wide blue and white floral border, plus blue and white fringing to tone in with the colour scheme.

First make a plain blue valance to hide the bed base. The bedspread is a luxury touch. This should hang to floor level and should be fitted neatly round the posts at the base of the bed so that it hangs smoothly. For a real 17th century effect, make it in alternate wide stripes of plain fabric and border, running the whole length of the bed, over the blankets from pillow to floor level at the foot of the bed. Edge the bedspread with blue and white fringe.

Hang matching curtains at the four corners of the bed to cover the posts. In the 17th century, these would be drawn at night to enclose the bed, but modern hangings need only be wide enough to give a draped effect round the outside of the posts. Hang the curtains from a rail fixed to the tester frame.

Make the curtains from the plain blue fabric, with vertical borders of the blue and white patterned fabric down both sides of each curtain. Again use the blue and white fringe to edge the curtain hem, which should be about 8in. up from the floor. Cover the tester with a deep straight pelmet, with no gathers. This would be most effective in alternate vertical bands of plain blue fabric and border.

Continue the blue and white theme with the bedroom chairs. These can be wooden ones with turned legs, upholstered in the plain blue fabric, with the seat edged by the blue and white fringe. The chair legs could be painted blue to match the fabric, or polished to their natural colour.

The dressing table is a particularly attractive idea and easy to make. It is a plain square wooden table (an old kitchen table from a junk shop would be an inexpensive buy). Cover it with a fitted floor-length table cloth, using the plain blue fabric. Edge the hem with the blue and white fringe and decorate the seams at the corners with a white braid to look like frog fastenings. A glass top over the cloth is a good idea for protection. Fix a small mirror to the wall above the dressing table; this could have a lacquered or marquetry frame.

The bedroom walls would have been covered with a blue and white fabric, so choose a wallpaper in a blue and white floral pattern that looks like fabric. The 17th century pattern could have been a bold one and it is possible to find a good modern paper that has the same effect. Some of the older wallpaper manufacturers reproduce period patterns.

An effective idea is to use the wallpaper to make the door into a concealed one. Cover the door with a flat piece of hardboard and then paper it to match the wall. The architrave should also be papered to match so the whole door 'disappears' into the walls. Other paintwork could be white, with white shutters at the windows and a parquet floor. However, a fitted carpet would be a warmer answer and would not detract from the period effect of the room.

A Spanish 17th century bedroom would also be attractive. It is possible to buy reproduction Spanish beds with elaborately turned posts, based on the old designs. Make a fitted bed-spread with gathered skirts to floor level. If you choose a four-poster, edge the tester with a gathered pelmet. Choose, perhaps, velvet for the tester, edged with braid, and a period-style flowered chintz for the bedspread. Cover the floor with vinyl sheeting or tiles to look like ceramic flooring. There are some excellent Spanish-style traditional patterns available. Then add a colourful Spanish rug.

It was a Spanish and Portuguese fashion to paper the walls up to dado (waist) level, then paint the upper parts of the walls in a plain white. This is an extremely attractive idea for a bedroom and is fairly easy to do. Choose a bold period-style paper that looks like fabric, in a sweeping Baroque design. Use this paper up to waist level on all the walls, then paint the upper part of the wall white. Fix a band of border paper horizontally round the walls at waist level to neaten the top of the wallpaper. Add brass lanterns or wall sconces, then two tall candles on the dressing table, and the effect is completed.

Below. *This living room, with its panelled walls, stone fireplace and polished wood floors, is typical of the period. Note the gate-leg table and tapestry seat covers.*

THE NATIONAL TRUST/JOHN BETHELL

Above. This Adam dining room illustrates a typical scheme using many pastel shades. The pictures were painted specially for the room.

The period touch— the eighteenth century: 1

This chapter moves on to the Georgian period, and outlines the main developments in interior design during the 18th century. It deals with the styles popular in France during the reigns of Louis XIV and XV, and highlights the influence they had on English and American furnishings. There are details about the great interior designers and cabinet makers, whose names are now associated with the Regency period.

The eighteenth century was an era of superb craftsmanship. Designers and cabinet makers produced furniture and houses that were beautifully thought out and constructed. It was also an era of elegant living, so the homes of the fashion followers in the 18th century reflected this in their design and interior decoration. A wide range of different materials was used to create sumptuous interiors. Paintings, mirrors, gilt, silks, satins and rich tapestries were combined to create beautiful rooms with intricate plasterwork decorations to offset the fine furniture.

France was the main influence on interior design, particularly during the early part of the 18th century. Louis XIV's Palace of Versailles was a showpiece, famed throughout Europe. The style which developed in France during the early part of the century was known as *Régence*. The grand and often heavy baroque ideas of the 17th century had gradually developed into a lighter and more elegant style.

French Régence style

Court life was sophisticated and the trend setters of the age sought informal surroundings with an intimate atmosphere in their homes. They built houses with two or three grand rooms for entertaining and small private apartments on the other floors. They created comfortable bedrooms, salons and boudoirs.

Being on a smaller scale than in previous centuries, these rooms needed to be furnished with smaller furniture, so craftsmen began to create newer and much more compact furniture. That is why much 18th century style furniture can be fitted so smartly into modern homes. Furniture design became more delicate with elegant curves. Rich bronze mounts, decorative inlays and veneers were used to add interest to the furniture, particularly in France.

Commodes were a fashionable invention of early 18th century furniture designers. These were beautifully made chests of drawers, which usually had two or three long drawers, a marble top and short, curved legs. They often had curved or 'serpentine' fronts and were decorated with gilt-bronze mounts and beautiful marquetry work. These would be used in sitting rooms, dining rooms and bedrooms.

Large writing tables also became fashionable. Known as a 'bureau plat', a typical one would have four curved legs, three drawers in a row under the large table top, and again bronze mounts and inlays or marquetry decoration. The centre drawer would be recessed a little to make it comfortable for sitting at.

Chairs were much more comfortable than before. These usually had elegant curved 'cabriole' legs. The seat fabric would be changed to suit the season or fashion. A lighter fabric would be used in summer and a heavier one in winter. This probably seems an extravagant idea but two sets of seat covers and even curtains is a good idea for a room because they last much longer. This would not be expensive for people who make their own chair covers and curtains. It would also make it possible to change the whole character of a room quickly without going through a complete redecoration process.

Women began to wear large wide skirts again, and chairs had shorter arms that did not stretch the full side length, so as to make room for the skirts. Canework also became popular once more and was used frequently on chair backs and seats as well as on chaises-longues.

Painted furniture also came back into fashion, and a typical bedroom would have the wooden bed frame painted to match the walls. The upholstery, bed hangings and curtains would all be in a matching fabric. This idea would be quite easy to copy.

Rococo style in France

When Louis XV came to the throne, furniture and interior styles had developed into what is known as Rococo. Swirling designs were full of curves and richly embellished with shells, flowers, foliage, scrolls and strange masks or animals. More new furniture was designed for

the fashion-conscious who lived a highly sophisticated life.

There were thickly cushioned settees, deep winged armchairs, ornamental cabinets for storage and display of precious knick-knacks, fire screens, commodes with doors, and corner cupboards. Nearly all the table-level furniture was fitted with marble tops. There were small occasional tables, and one of the most popular pieces was a toilet table. These were elaborately designed with all manner of drawers, sectioned off to hold the huge assortment of powders and toilet requisites. Some would have flap tops with mirrors inside, others would be dual-purpose desks-cum-toilet tables.

The cabinet makers of the day put a great deal of ingenuity into making what were then considered highly necessary pieces of furniture. The writing table or desk was also considered vital. Many beautiful designs appeared and intricate pieces of furniture were created for the purpose. Most furniture was heavily ornamented, and some of the designs tended to be frivolous rather than functional.

Comparatively little fashionable French furniture remains from the middle and last half of the 18th century because so much was destroyed during the French Revolution. What does appear on the market is highly priced and usually bought by museums or people with good financial resources. However, many of the less elaborate designs are still made by reproduction furniture makers, and these are the ones which

can be used successfully if you want to create a feeling of 18th century France in your home. Add to the effect by cunning use of colour and soft furnishings.

Chinese style

Oriental themes were highly popular, both in England and on the Continent as well as in America. There was not enough true Oriental lacquer available to meet the great demand for lacquered furniture, so the French and English made their own. This usually had a white or coloured background, which was a contrast to the true Oriental lacquer, which had a dark background. The lacquer work was used for panels in cabinets, and Oriental styling became popular for wallpapers, fabric design and carving on furniture.

Louis XVI

This French King's reign began in 1771 and heralded another change in fashion. These were the years of ostentatious and sumptuous living which ended abruptly with the French Revolution. Design reflected the way of life, with extravagantly decorated and rich-looking furniture and houses that cost a fortune.

French cabinet makers were famous all over Europe, and their styles were copied and furniture bought by other countries. Designs became less curvaceous than in the Rococo period, and furniture would have straight rather than curved legs, but the embellishments were as rich as ever. Plaques of Sèvres porcelain were inset into furniture for decoration. Another popular form of decoration was mahogany veneer. The wood used for this came from the base of the tree trunk because it was richly patterned with curves and knots, which looked attractive when used as veneers on cabinet doors etc.

The end of the 18th century in France was a period of transition in furniture design, after the upheaval of the Revolution. It was the beginnings of the Directoire style, which later became universally popular. But the furniture during this particular period tended to be much more formal, and was sometimes based on the Neo-Classical English designs by Adam and Chippendale.

Left. This rich-looking room reflects 18th century classical taste, particularly the pier glass between the windows and the arrangement of paintings. The silk velvet on the walls is original. Below. The panelled walls of this early 18th century living room were painted later. The pink curtains and sofa cover give a good colour combination, and the comfortable chair makes this an elegant yet homely room.

The period style in England

At the beginning of the 18th century, England tended to follow the French ideas, but later in the century the English style came into its own and the beautiful work of Adam and Chippendale became popular in many other countries including America.

Architects were the main influence on design in 18th century homes. They not only designed the house exteriors, but planned complete interiors down to carpets, furniture and door knobs as well.

Design took on a Classical feeling, and beautifully proportioned Palladian-style homes were built. Lord Burlington and William Kent were the first and most famous exponents of this style during that period. The concept of these elegant houses was based on designs by Palladio, an Italian Renaissance architect.

Everything was much more restrained in England than in France, with modestly furnished, though elegant houses. This classical styling produced practical Georgian houses almost totally without washing facilities. These design ideas are popular with today's architects who create Georgian-style homes on a more compact scale with well-fitted modern kitchens

and bathrooms. Both this chapter and the next one will help those of you with homes of this type to create a true Georgian touch for their homes.

The Rococo movement in France soon began to have its followers in England, and the flowing designs embellished with scrolls and flowers began to appear on gold and silverware and on stucco work and carvings in houses. Furniture design was slower to take up the theme, and really successful Rococo furniture did not appear until the 1740s.

At the same time there was a revival of the Mediaeval Gothic architectural style for interior and exterior design. The most famous example is Horace Walpole's fantasy villa at Strawberry Hill, Twickenham, Middlesex. It has amazingly embellished ceilings which can still be seen today. Here, and with other houses during this period, the Gothic theme was handled lightly, making colourful homes that were full of character. This was a complete contrast to the heavy Gothic styles of the much later Victorian era.

Thomas Chippendale

The most famous cabinet maker and furniture designer of the period was Thomas Chippendale, and his elegant styles are still being faithfully copied by reproduction furniture makers. He published a unique book of furniture designs which is an excellent record of the fashionable furniture designs of his day. Unlike the French, who decorated so much of their furniture with bronze and gilt, Chippendale relied mainly on carving to add interest to his designs.

He designed beautiful 'chinoiserie' chairs in the Oriental style, often with legs and backs carved to look like bamboo. He made a fantastic Gothic bed with an elaborately carved tester that looked like a crown. There were curving Rococo commodes, tables and decorative smaller items like mirrors and candlestands, all beautifully carved.

Robert Adam

The last half of the 18th century saw the growth of Neo-Classicism. The main setter of this style was the famous architect Robert Adam, who had studied in Rome. Adam used the design ideas of Ancient Rome as his inspiration. His styles were formal and grand, though they can be used today on a much smaller scale to conjure up beautiful period-style rooms.

Adam designed furniture, accessories, interiors and exteriors, so his houses had a total look. He was as revolutionary an influence on 18th century house fashions in England as Mary Quant was on clothes in the 1950s.

Painted furniture became popular once more. Adam would arrange formal groups of furniture together in a symmetrical way. A typical idea of his was a dining room arrangement for a sideboard. There would be a long side table for serving with urns or pedestals on either side. Beneath the table was a wine cooler and often on either side of it tall and elaborately made jugs.

Although many of Adam's Neo-Classical designs seem closely related to the French Louis XVI ones, the French did not adopt the classical styles until some years after Adam had begun his work on this theme.

Hepplewhite and Sheraton

Adam's furniture designs and ideas were translated by George Hepplewhite and Thomas Sheraton, two famous designers and cabinet makers. They both published books of their designs which were famous in their day. Chippendale, also, was an exponent of Adam's Neo-Classical style.

Colours and wallcoverings

Adam favoured pastel colours, and the rooms he created would often combine two shades of pale blue with white or pastel pink and white. Pink and pale green was another popular colour combination, and the colours were always fresh-looking. In the grander homes, gold leaf was used to pick out the elegant plasterwork. Fabrics were rich and popular ones were moiré, brocade, satin and silk. Houses had large windows with long curtains which had elaborately draped pelmets.

Chinese hand-painted wallpapers were one of the most fashionable wallcoverings. Machines for printing wallpaper were invented during the late 18th century, so it became much more widely available. Painted wall panels were another popular way of decorating a room and elaborate crystal chandeliers were the most fashionable form of lighting.

The elegant English style became fashionable on the Continent, particularly in Italy, Germany, Holland, Scandinavia and Spain. In these countries, chairs were designed and made, particularly in the styles of Chippendale, Hepplewhite and Sheraton.

American style in the 18th century shows how the fashions followed those in England. The beginning of the century saw the transatlantic version of William and Mary, then later on Queen Anne styles, followed by the Rococo fashions of the 'American Chippendale' period. Settlers in America brought the furnishing and architectural styles of their countries with them. This will be dealt with in greater detail in a later chapter.

It is interesting that furniture making was regarded purely as a luxury trade in France and her European neighbours, while in England and America it was not. Town and rural furniture-making was much more closely related, which makes many of the less elaborate ideas so easy to recreate today. For instance, the Windsor chair was a famous 18th century invention. It was made in great numbers in the 18th century and is still being made today with the design virtually unchanged.

All this information on the development of furniture making and interior styles will help you to get a good idea of what was popular in the particular period that interests you, so you will be able to translate the ideas for yourself.

Top picture. This early 18th century living room shows how panelling was painted and outlined with crisp white paint. The period portraits and arrangement of antique furniture round the room complete the scene. Centre. A fine four-poster bed with hangings to match the curtains dominates this panelled bedroom. Bottom. The neo-Gothic style was used in this mid-18th century living room, with its elaborate vaulted ceiling with fan tracery.

THE NATIONAL TRUST/JOHN BETHELL

JOHN BETHELL

16

The period touch—the eighteenth century: 2

Of all the many period styles, Georgian ones are among the easiest to translate. The fresh-looking colours and elegant furniture look good in even the smallest of homes. This chapter has specific advice and ideas for giving an 18th century look to a house exterior and a bedroom.

The Georgian style was a total look, and architects designed not only the house exteriors, but also complete interior schemes and furniture. While it is relatively simple to achieve a Georgian flavour inside your home, you may also find that the Georgian look can be given to the exterior. Dull turn-of-the-century terraced houses take on a new lease of life when they are given careful Georgian treatment.

The exterior

If you like the idea of giving your house-front a Georgian face-lift, you will find it quite easy. The art of a successful treatment of this type is not to overdo it. Plain 1900s style terraced cottages lend themselves well to this type of treatment, often because the Georgian-style windows give them better proportions.

Below. *The stucco fronts of this Georgian terrace have been painted in the same colour, which gives them a smart uniform appearance.*

BLUE CIRCLE GROUP/LONDON BOROUGH OF CAMDEN

The first step is to work out a colour scheme for the house front. Georgian-style houses often had stucco fronts, and these were painted white or in a pastel colour, pink being one of the most popular choices. Alternatively they had brick or stone fronts which were left unpainted so the natural colour could be appreciated. If yours is a basically dark-looking terraced house, a bright coat of paint for the whole house front would probably be the best answer.

The next step is to alter the windows so that they suit the period. Rather than have two large panes of glass for a big sash window, Georgian ones had twelve or so smaller panes of glass in each window. Many builder's merchants sell Georgian style windows which are ideal for the purpose. Fit this type instead of existing windows to conjure up more of a Georgian feeling. Bow windows are another alteration to make and can often be successful in adding the right atmosphere. Bow windows look most attractive in older houses with the balanced architecture of the Georgian style. Fitting is also really quite simple, but if in doubt consult a manual. Once they are fitted, paint the frames white.

The front door also needs to suit the Georgian style, with smart-looking panels, a shining brass door knob, knocker and bell pull. Here again, it is easy to buy doors of this style from builders' merchants if your existing front door looks wrong. Georgian doors were often painted white or in bright colours. Sometimes the beading on the door panels was picked out in a contrasting colour.

Use a narrow paint brush and you will find this work is easy to do. There are a number of gadgets on the market, which are useful for this work. Choose a colour scheme to match the house front. For a white house front a good colour scheme could be a Wedgwood blue door with the beading picked out in white. Other ideas are dark blue or maroon doors with white beading; a white door with maroon beading; an Adam green door with white beading.

It is important that the door architrave should suit the period style. Grander doors were often flanked by columns, however this type of treatment may be too overpowering for a small cottage, where a plainer architrave would be more in keeping.

It is sometimes possible to buy actual Georgian doors from houses that are being demolished, and in this case it is worth stripping off the paint to get back to the natural wood colour. You may be lucky enough to find you have a beautiful door of seasoned mahogany which can then be finished with a shining seal for a highly polished woodgrain finish—also popular in Georgian days.

The final touches are the brass knob and knocker. There are plenty of reproduction ones on the market. Alternatively try searching round antique and junk shops for the real thing.

In the bedroom

Bedrooms lend themselves particularly well to this style. Built-in beds had always been popular and in this era they were designed in an attractive way that is easy to copy. Here is an idea for a Louis XV style bedroom, with a draped bed built into an alcove.

Panelled rooms were the most fashionable idea in the Louis XV era and it would not be difficult to get a panelled effect in the bedroom. Tack strips of decorative beading to the walls in rectangular shapes so they look like panels. For extra decoration use flower and garland shapes, made from plastic. These are made in period styles and are available from most DIY shops. They can be used to decorate the corners or centres of the 'panels'.

After fixing the panels and their decoration, paint the walls and ceiling in the same colour. To get the best effect, study books with illustrations of period rooms beforehand, so you are able to work out a genuine-looking design for the imitation panels and decorative work.

An original Louis XV panelled bedroom would be designed with an alcove large enough to take the bed longways so it did not stick out into the centre of the room. Unless there is an existing room in your house with a bed-sized alcove, the best way of getting the effect would be to make a false alcove for the bed. Do this by building out floor-to-ceiling fitted cupboards at either end of the bed, so it appears to be made to measure in its own little niche. Add a deep plywood pelmet above the bed to make a smooth line between the cupboard fronts. For added effect the pelmet could have a curved shape.

The fitted cupboards will need to be as deep as the bed is wide—so this plan would not really be practical for a double bed. Work out a design plan with the bed along the centre of a long wall and a tall cupboard at each end joined at the top by the pelmet.

Choose panelled doors for the cupboards. Depending on the size of the bedroom, you

Below. Modern neo-Georgian terraced house exteriors have a lot of scope for being re-vamped to give them a more authentic look and emphasize their period features.

could have double or single cupboard doors at each end of the bed. Fix architraves round the doors for added effect. If there is a top cupboard above the doors, make this into a 'concealed' one so it appears to be part of the wall. Edge the door with a decorative beading to match the panelled effect in the rest of the room.

If you choose a wallpaper instead of the panelling idea, paper the top cupboard door so that it 'disappears' into the rest of the wallpaper pattern. The easiest way to do this is to paper straight over the door and walls together, then when the paper is dry use a sharp knife to cut a neat line round the edge of the door so it can be opened.

Once the cupboards and alcove are completed, alter the cornice so it comes across the top of the new row of cupboards and the linking pelmet. This makes a much more professional job of the 'built-in' idea. A Louis XV cornice would be elaborate, so you may find you need to add extra beading or to put in a new cornice altogether. Decorative coving can be done by any handyman and different materials are available. Builder's merchants usually stock cornices in different period styles, so it should be fairly easy to find a suitable one.

A typical Louis XV bed would have head- and foot-boards of carved gilt. Elaborate bedheads can often be found in junk shops. They are most likely to be Victorian ones of mahogany. If the design seems suitably ornate, use bedheads of this type which can be painted to look like gilt.

The bed hangings complete the effect. Cover the walls and ceiling in the new bed alcove with fabric to match the curtains and bedspread or use a matching wallpaper. The use of fabrics to cover walls gives a total textured look to the room. Make rich looking curtains in the bed fabric and hang these so they frame the bed. They can be hung on a modern curtain rail which

will be concealed by the pelmet across the bed alcove.

Catch the curtains back in graceful folds held in place by loops of braid with decorative tassels. Make a plain fitted cover for the bed in the same fabric as the curtains. For a richer effect this can be decorated with braid round the hem and edges of the bed. If the room is a bed-sitter, the curtains can be drawn across the bed alcove during the daytime so that the bed is concealed.

Use period-style furniture in the rest of the room with a small polished occasional table for a lamp by the bed. Scout round antique shops and reproduction furniture stockists for a 'toilet table' which can be used as a dressing table. Choose a Louis XV style chair that has curved legs and arms painted gilt, with an upholstered seat and back, covered in a material to match the bed.

At the windows hang long curtains to match the bed hangings. A small gilt chandelier would make the best choice for lighting. For extra storage space, choose a small commode with two drawers and curved legs. A large gilt-framed mirror on the wall would be another good accessory. Add period-style pictures and ornaments—Chinese vases were the most popular choice in Louis XV's time.

A good colour scheme would be deep pink or crimson, white and gold. Choose pink coloured damask, brocade or silk-type fabric for the bed, curtains and upholstery. Paint the walls, woodwork and ceiling white, perhaps with the beading picked out in gilt.

A much simpler version would be to make an 18th century Swedish-style alcove bed. One like this can be seen in Gripsholm Castle, Sweden. The alcove for the bed is surrounded with a plain architrave and the drapes are of boldly checked linen. A shaped linen pelmet is stretched across the top of the alcove and behind it are plain floor-length curtains of matching fabric, caught back with loops made in the same fabric.

The bed has a plain wooden frame which is padded and upholstered with the linen fabric. Nearby is a turned wooden chair upholstered in the checked linen. Instead of being covered with fabric to match the bed, the walls throughout the room, and in the bed alcove, are hung with 'panels' of softly patterned fabric. The paintwork is plain with the beading picked out in a contrasting colour. Apple green and white would be a bright colour scheme for a room of this type. Choose white paintwork, with the beading picked out in apple green, plus green and white gingham fabric for the bed and hangings and upholstery.

You could make the wall 'panels' yourself from creamy white linen or heavy cotton satin. Cut out the panels to size first and turn under the raw edges. Now paint on a leafy border

Above left. *This bed has been constructed under the eaves in an attic room, with a cupboard built in to fill the alcove. The gold colour scheme is most effective.*
Left. *A headboard panel covered in fabric to match the bedspread gives this bedroom a Georgian feeling. The fireplace, painting and antique furniture complete the theme.*

design, using a fabric dye paint. Leaves are quite easy for an amateur to paint, and the pattern should be a delicate one. This is fun to do and is a splendid way of making your own fabric design.

If you don't want a complete period-style bedroom, it is fun to make a small corner with an 18th century effect. One of the most attractive ideas of the Chippendale era was to have a draped dressing table. This went well with the four-poster beds that were popular in those days.

The dressing table is easy to make and does not involve buying expensive antique or reproduction furniture. Portraits of the 1750s and 1760s sometimes showed ladies at their dressing tables and it would be simple to copy a design from one of these. Here is one way : first choose a plain rectangular table. This is to be covered with lace skirts and a gathered pelmet. A mirror stands on the table and this is also draped, rather like a cot canopy, with attractive lace curtains that frame the mirror and curve over the sides of the table to floor-level.

Above. *This delicately carved four-poster bed with chintz hangings gives an 18th century touch to this bedroom, painted in a soft apricot. The footstool, lamps and bedside tables add to the period flavour.*

First make a plain lining cloth for the table as a 'petticoat' for the lace skirts. Choose either white or a pastel colour—an old sheet would be an inexpensive choice. Choose a white or cream coloured decorative lace for the draperies. Terylene and nylon lace fabrics are effective and wash well, or cotton lace is a good choice. Make gathered skirts of the lace for the dressing table. Choose a 5 or 6in. deep lace border to make a gathered pelmet round the edge of the table top. This pelmet and the skirts beneath could be attached with Velcro so they are easy to remove for washing.

Cover the table top with a plain white fabric which can be protected with a sheet of glass. Choose a fairly ornate mirror with a gilt surround and then make the drapes for this from two

long lengths of lace which are tightly gathered together in the middle and decorated with a big moiré bow over the top of the mirror where they are secured, giving almost the effect of a crown. Arrange the drapes on either side of the mirror, so they curve gently to the table edge and reach to floor level. Add two more moiré bows to the curves on either side of the mirror as extra rich decoration. The far edges of the drapes should be joined down the centre behind the mirror.

On the dressing table, place two brass candlesticks and a collection of old scent bottles for effect (these are easy to find in antique or junk shops). The finished dressing table is as feminine as can be and most attractive. A practical idea would be to fix the drapes in the front of the table on to a concealed door, so you could fix drawers underneath for cosmetics etc.

Having studied the illustrations on these pages and bearing in mind some of these ideas for 18th century style bedrooms, you should have an enjoyable time creating a period style bedroom of your choice.

The period touch— Eighteenth century living rooms and dining rooms

Georgian interior design and architecture were fully described in the two previous chapters, and there have been ideas for giving a period touch to a house exterior and a bedroom. This article tells how to give an 18th century touch to a living room and dining room in a modern house.

Above. *The Adam mantelpiece, decorative cornice, panelling and arched recess give this living room an attractive 18th century appearance. The elegant antique furniture and soft colours complete the effect.*

Elegance was the order of the day in a mid-18th century living room. The Adam style is one of the best on which to base a room scheme, mainly because it is much more restrained than the French fashions of the same time, and therefore easier to imitate.

Before you begin, try to visit an Adam-style house or look through a book with illustrations of Georgian houses and interiors, also study the pictures in this and the previous two chapters carefully so that you know what colours, fabric patterns and furniture styles to choose.

BRIAN MORRIS

In the living room

If you decide to give your living room an 18th century look, you should start by choosing a colour scheme. White and gold would be a good basic one, with crimson or fresh lime green for the furnishing fabrics.

Many of the houses Adam designed had ceilings beautifully decorated with moulded plasterwork and carpets woven specially so that the floor pattern matched the ceiling pattern. This is obviously on too expensive a scale for a small modern home, so how do you sift through the grander ideas and end up with an unusual room that cleverly catches the flavour of Adam's Neo-Classical style? One of the best ways is to conjure up a period atmosphere in the structure of the room. Combined with a good colour scheme and period style furnishings, the finished result will be effective.

First, work on the cornice. An Adam house would have a decorative cornice, so you could make more of your existing one by making it deeper. Buy Adam-style medallions or flower motifs made from plastic to look like the original plaster mouldings and designed to embellish

furniture. Attach a row of these all the way round the top of the room about 5in. below the cornice. Below these add a moulded picture rail, so that the medallions are equidistant between the top of the rail and the bottom of the cornice. Paint everything—i.e. picture rail, ceiling, cornice and mouldings in white, then pick out the medallions in gold.

The fireplace was an important feature and made a striking focal point in the original rooms of this period. Adam-style fireplaces are popular to this day, so they can be found in many specialist shops or through builders' merchants. So change your existing fireplace for one of these, with elegant side columns and an attractive mantelpiece. The original ones were usually made either in carved marble or carved wood which was then painted to match the rest of the room.

Install the new fireplace with an open grate and in this put a period-style fire-back and fire basket. These are sometimes to be found in antique shops or reproduction ones can be obtained through good ironmongers' shops. It is also possible to buy electric or gas fires which

22

of the curtain. As extra decoration you could edge the pelmet with a deep gold fringe and matching braid.

Alternatively, ruched blinds were popular in Georgian days. These are quite fiddly to make, but look stunning and help enormously to give a good atmosphere. You need a plain silky fabric as wide as the window and twice as long; a floor-length blind would be most effective. Make vertical gathering stitches in three evenly-spaced rows, and gather the edges also. Pull the gathering stitches up until the blind is the right length to cover the window. Now overstitch all the rows of gathering so that it does not lose its shape. When hung the gathers will give a richly scalloped effect.

Attach pulls like those on a concertina blind Ruched blinds work in the same way. These are plastic rings sewn in rows up the gathers on the reverse side of the blinds. Run pull cords up each row of gathering through the rings, with a pulling mechanism at the side, so that the blind can be lifted evenly. Add a deep fringe to the bottom edge of the blind.

The final touch is to add a carved pelmet that sets off the top of the blind, but this is an optional idea. A typical Chippendale pelmet would be carved to look like actual draped fabric, then painted gold. To get the effect, search in junk shops for a strip of carving or a large ornate picture frame that could be adapted to look like a pelmet.

Choose period-style furnishings upholstered to match the wallpaper and curtains—armchairs and settees with painted legs, and comfortably cushioned. A writing table is one attractive piece of furniture to choose. For lighting, use a glass chandelier (small period-style ones can be found in most good furnishing shops). Final touches are mirrors and pictures in Adam-style gold frames. Porcelain figures became fashionable towards the end of the 18th century and would be a good choice as ornaments.

Efficient modern storage units are now being made with period styling. Although furniture of this particular type was not invented in Adam's day, a well-designed period-style unit in a deep-coloured wood like mahogany could be useful in a living room where storage space is so often at a premium. One particular design that is internationally available has Hepplewhite styling.

Alternative decoration ideas would be to have a French-style room with a richly coloured flock wallpaper and printed chintz curtains. The chairs could be covered in a tapestry-like fabric or in a silky looking one. For lighting, choose an 18th century style carved wooden chandelier with a gilded frame.

To get the right period touch, it is interesting to note how furniture was grouped in 18th century rooms. Furniture was usually arranged symmetrically and tended to be placed round the walls of the room in large formal homes. A typical Neo-Classical group, which would look smart for a corner in a living room, would be to have a small semi-circular side table against the wall. On either side of it would be a pair of Chippendale-style chairs, upholstered in perhaps clear yellow or lime green silk. Above the table on the wall would be an oval mirror in a carved gilt frame. On the table there might be two small

Above left. The ornate plasterwork ceiling and frieze are typical of an Adam living room, also the draped pelmets. **Left.** The marble mantelpiece is the focal point of this living room, where paper borders define wall areas. **Above.** The deep blue walls highlight the mantelpiece and panelling in this living room, and act as an effective background for the mirror and ornaments. The furniture is also in keeping with the Georgian theme.

have a period-style surround that looks like a Georgian fire basket, and these would be useful for a room without a chimney.

Adam doorways usually had beautiful carved architraves. Catch the atmosphere by painting the existing architrave white, which makes a smart surround for a panelled door with a woodgrain finish. Use the existing door if it is suitable, otherwise scout round old houses and builders' merchants for one that will look right.

Strip off all the paint and give the door a polished mahogany look. If it is a deal or pine door, use a good quality wood stain to make the wood a rich brown colour, then finish with a

varnish or colourless polyurethane seal for a highly polished effect. Add period style brass door knobs and finger plates.

For the walls, use a formal silky-looking wallpaper that resembles damask, in a crimson or lime green colour. Choose floor-length curtains in a matching fabric or in plain white, decorated with gold braid. The curtains should be lined and interlined so that they hang well and look heavy. For extra effect make a draped pelmet from a width of the curtain fabric that measures the same length as the width of the window.

First fit a plywood frame over the curtain heading to support the pelmet. The frame should be about 6in. deep in front and flat on top so that the pelmet fabric can be tacked evenly to it. The frame should not be visible underneath the pelmet fabric. Line the length of fabric for the pelmet and turn under the raw edges. Stretch the fabric over the top of the pelmet frame and tack it down. Make the draped effect by stitching the pelmet fabric with a row of vertical gathering stitches in two places so that the fabric falls in a rich curve over the centre top of the window. It will then drape itself into points at each side vases. This basically simple symmetrical arrangement would be easy to make with reproduction furniture or antiques that you have discovered and renovated.

In the dining room

A formal Georgian dining room can be one of the most attractive rooms in the house, if you use period style furniture and a colour scheme that is typical of the era.

Use a similar cornice to the one suggested for the living room, this time decorated with garlands. Concentric circles of plaster moulding were sometimes used to decorate ceilings, and you may be lucky enough to find a builders' merchant who stocks moulding of this type. You could then make an Adam-style ceiling with a moulding in the centre to hold a chandelier and three or four larger circles of moulding outside it.

It was fashionable in the 18th century to treat pictures and mirrors as part of the wall, so they looked as if they were let into the wall with frames to match the decorative plaster mouldings in the rest of the room. This effect would be quite easy to conjure up in a dining room where it would look especially smart. Choose a large mirror to go over the fireplace and reproduction prints of favourite paintings of the period to hang on the other walls. Choose matching carved frames for the mirror and pictures and screw the frames to the wall, so they look as if they are part of it. As in the living room idea, choose an Adam-style fireplace as a focal point.

A typical Adam colour scheme would be two shades of pale blue with white. Paint the ceiling in the two shades of pale blue, with the darker shade—a Wedgwood blue would be an ideal colour—in the centre circle, and the paler toning shade round the outside circle. Paint the walls in the paler blue and the strip between the cornice and picture rail in the darker blue.

Paint everything else white, including the cornice, skirting, all decorative mouldings, fireplace, window frames and doors. This colour scheme is a beautiful one to choose for a dining room, and it looks fresh and inviting. Paint the doors white, with the panels and some of the beading picked out in blue to match the walls.

Choose long floor-length curtains in a plain pale blue silky fabric or a flower pattern that emphasizes the colour of the room. Original 18th century patterns are still being reproduced by some of the older-established fabric manufacturers, so it should not be difficult to find a suitable one. Either make curtains with plain headings and hang them from wooden rings on a big wooden or gilt pole. Alternatively decorate the curtains with a fringed and scalloped pelmet in the same fabric. You can use a plain pelmet but the more elaborate styles are more in keeping with the period.

Choose a brass or crystal chandelier hanging from the centre of the ceiling for lighting. For flooring, choose either parquet or plain stripped and sealed boards. Look for Georgian-style decanters to decorate the sideboard and Wedgwood vases for the mantelpiece. Another excellent addition to the room would be a long case clock. These were popular at that time and are made in reproduction styles. They can also be found in old furniture emporia.

A good alternative idea for a dining room

BRIAN MORRIS

PAUL REDMAN

decoration scheme is to use a frieze or border paper to give a panelled effect. First paint the room in the colour of your choice, or use a plain silk-effect wallpaper. Then stick the border paper over the top in rectangular shapes to make the panels. Join the border paper at the corners of the 'panels' with a neat 45° mitre cut. Some papers of this type come with special square pieces for finishing the corners neatly. Frieze or border papers can also be used to give a decorative effect round the top of the walls just below the cornice, and look effective in an

Top. This dining room, with its crystal chandelier, draped pelmet and parquet floor, is typical of the period. Above. The rich red walls highlight the Georgian features in this dining room. Note the carved mantelpiece and cornice, and gilt-framed painting and mirror.

Adam-style pattern if they are used in this way.

All these ideas should give you a good basis to work from, so that you are able to create unusual rooms with a sophisticated 18th century atmosphere.

The period touch— early American homes

TRANSWORLD/AMERICAN HOME

Towards the middle of the eighteenth century, the design styles popular in Europe had a great influence on the early settlers in North America and Canada. This chapter describes the developments in interior design during the Colonial and Federal areas, and has ideas on how to give an early American look to a modern dining room, bedroom and living room.

Early American and Canadian interiors and furnishing fashions resembled those of the settlers' mother countries. So while Virginia, New England, Pennsylvania and the Eastern Coast of the USA reflected English ideas; Canada, Louisiana, Maine and Wisconsin reflected French ideas; then New York, part of Pennsylvania and New Jersey followed Dutch fashions.

The early settlers built small and simple homes, furnished with only the bare necessities. Chests were important for storage, and among the most famous surviving examples of early styles are the Pennsylvania chests, decorated with paintings and stencils. These were in fact dower chests, made by German farmers for their daughters. Connecticut chests are also famous, and these were made by the settlers who decorated them with unusual carved sunflowers.

Extending tables were considered to be useful pieces of furniture in the early settlers' homes, and gate-leg tables were particularly popular. In Connecticut, the 'butterfly' table was invented; this had slanting legs and a folding top with supports shaped like butterfly wings.

England was the main influence on design for many years, so it is possible to see early Colonial furniture based on Jacobean, William and Mary and Queen Anne styles. The later American Federal styles were based mainly on the ideas of English Georgian and Regency and French Empire.

All these styles were popular later on than in England because fashions travelled slowly. However, American furniture was never quite as ornamented as European. The designs were translated in slightly more simplified terms, so the furnishing fashions were usually more restrained than in Europe. It is as if American craftsmen, most of whom went over as settlers, took a close look at the fashions of their mother countries and then emphasized the best of each particular style without overdoing it.

Dutch settlers, instead of using chests for storage, made large two-doored wardrobes. A typical one, known as a *kast*, would have a painted finish, decorated with still-life pictures of fruit and flowers.

A strictly religious group called the Shakers made some of the earliest original American furniture. Their movement had developed from the English Quakers. During the late 18th and early 19th centuries they made beautiful rustic furniture of simple design, with straight, clean lines, uncluttered by carving.

On a more elegant scale, the curved 'cabriole' legs that became fashionable in Queen Anne's

Left. A good example of an early American dining room, with its open fireplace and beamed ceiling. The simple furniture and copper and pewter ware add authenticity.

CLIVE CORLESS

tion. This was closely paralleled by English Regency styles, which also influenced American ideas.

In the past, American cabinet makers had tended to copy European fashions in a lighter way, but during the late Federal period, the furniture tended to be heavier than its original counterpart. Even so, some beautiful furniture and elegant homes were created.

Fashionable decoration ideas varied from region to region. Furniture was often painted or decorated with marquetry and veneers, and canework was also popular. In Baltimore, for example, furniture was decorated with panels of gilt and painted glass. In Boston, fashions were influenced by Sheraton's ideas and furniture was decorated with beautifully grained veneers in many different woods.

There were many well-known furniture craftsmen whose work was sought after during the American Federal era. These included Samuel McIntire of Salem, who made fashionable tables and chairs, as well as designing houses. Philadelphia continued to be an important place for furniture, and two of the most famous cabinet makers there were Ephraim Haines and Henry Connelly. They followed Sheraton's Neo-Classical styles.

In New York, Duncan Phyfe, who had emigrated from Scotland, began by making furniture based on Sheraton's ideas. He later developed his own individual style, often making chairs with lyre-shaped backs. This idea was popular at the same time during the English Regency era.

day soon caught on in 18th century America. Different parts of America made their own distinctive versions of this particular fashion.

Upholstered settees and sofas became fashionable in the mid-18th century. Windsor chairs also became great favourites, especially in country homes. These were not as heavily constructed as the original English versions on which they were based. During the mid-18th century, furniture was often decorated with carved shells.

American Chippendale

Around 1760 Rococo styling and the designs of Chippendale reached America and were widely reproduced. They were popular for about 20 years. Furniture feet were decorated in the carved 'claw and ball' style, particularly in Philadelphia, which was one of the main centres for the craft of furniture making. Different features of Chippendale's designs influenced cabinet makers in different parts of America. The furniture was ideal for the elegant new homes that were being built at the time.

The American Federal era

The Federal fashions were the first furnishing and interior ideas to appear after the American Revolution and many of the designs were based on the French Empire and Directoire styles. The Federal style was popular from the end of the 18th century until well into the 19th century.

The early Federal furniture was based on Adam's Neo-Classical ideas and decorated with classical-looking columns and scroll work. Later on the Empire style was the main inspira-

Above. The handsome refectory table, ladder-back chairs and sideboard give this modern dining room a Colonial flavour. The antique cutlery box, gilt chandelier and iron candle holder complete the theme.
Below. A four-poster bed hung with fabric to match the curtains and an elegant chair enhance this Colonial-style bedroom.

Right. The early American country style has been retained in this attic bedroom, with its pitched ceiling, exposed rafters and bright rugs on the wood floor.
Far right. This comfortable living room in a modern house has been given a Federal touch. Note the plain white walls, heavy beamed ceiling and open fireplace.

DOUGLAS SIMMONDS

JANET AND FRANK BEYDA

TRANSWORLD/AMERICAN HOME

A French cabinet maker called Charles Honoré Lannuier worked in New York at the same time. His designs reflected the Empire styles that were popular in France.

Other crafts

Furniture making was not the only craft that developed greatly during the American Colonial and Federal eras. German-type glass making was carried out in Pennsylvania and New Jersey. Beautiful pottery and porcelain were made, particularly by Bonnin and Morris of Philadelphia, and the designs closely resembled European ones. Boston was the main centre for silver, and fashions followed the plain Georgian English designs.

English, French and Oriental carpets were imported and used in the grander homes. French Canadians originated the craft of home-made rugs from strips of cloth and wool hooked through tough canvas backing. These often had beautiful geometric or flower patterns and were used in many country homes. Another popular craft that developed during the late 18th century was that of making patchwork quilts. The original ideas had been brought over from England.

Achieving the period touch

Any of the ideas for making rooms in the 18th century style given in the last two chapters of this series would also apply to North America for the Federal style. Now that you have the background idea of what was used in the original settlers' homes, you can adapt the various ideas to suit your own home. Here are some fresh ideas for the three main rooms in the house to give you extra inspiration.

The rustic simplicity of the Colonial style is always popular, though original furniture of the period is now very scarce and mostly to be seen only in museums. However, good and reasonably inexpensive reproduction furniture is not difficult to come by, and an ever-watchful eye for junk shop bargains that can be renovated is a must for anyone who wants to try amd emulate a particular period style.

In the dining room

The dining room is one of the best rooms in the house for Colonial-style treatment. Usually the fireplace wall was panelled, while the other three walls were white plaster, and there would be a beamed ceiling. This effect is an attractive one to re-create. Colonial-style panelling on a

fireplace is simple to do. Remove the old chimneypiece and make a large open grate with a plain brick lining.

If your dining room is without a chimney, make a shallow false grate to get the effect and fix the panelled wall a foot inside the original wall to make room for the fake fireplace. If space is at a premium, cut unobtrusive doors in the panelling on each side of the fireplace and use the space behind for storing glasses etc on fitted shelves. Fix the doors on long black wrought iron hinges.

The old Colonial-style rooms did not usually have mantelpieces, so all you need to do is panel the entire fireplace wall with wide vertical strips of tongued and grooved pine or deal. This can then be stained slightly darker for added effect.

On a cheaper scale, you can use a good wallpaper that gives the effect of simple old panelling. In the fireplace use plain cast iron fire dogs, a fire back and pokers. Make the floor plain with sanded and sealed boards in a rich oak or nut brown colour.

Use a heavy refectory-style table with turned legs. A table of this type is easy and inexpensive for a do-it-yourself enthusiast to make. Search round furniture shops for plain dining chairs with cane seats. A heavy carved oak chest could be used as a dresser.

To complete the effect, search round junk shops for pewter candlesticks and plates as decoration in the room. An old cauldron in the fireplace would be another good touch. At the windows, use plain shutters made from vertical strips of tongued and grooved pine or deal, fixed on wrought iron hinges.

An Empire dining room would be equally effective to give the atmosphere of the American Federal period, but it would be on a more sophisticated scale. An ideal colour scheme that was popular at the time is royal blue, yellow and white. Start with yellow painted walls and ceiling, white woodwork and windows and a white cornice.

Choose curtains of richly patterned satiny fabric with a yellow background and royal blue pattern. Gather these richly and loop them on each side of the window. Make a pelmet in plain royal blue. Cut the base of the pelmet in a series of decorative V-shapes, all the same size, and bind the edge with plain yellow narrow braid. Cover the seats of the dining chairs with either the patterned fabric used for the curtains or a plain royal blue.

Empire-style fireplaces were usually elaborately carved marble. Try to approximate the style with a reproduction fireplace—glassfibre ones look quite effective, are reasonably inexpensive, and come in a wide range of period styles.

Choose mahogany furniture that blends with the period atmosphere of the room. A round dining room table would be ideal. Empire-style ones often had tops of inlaid marble. A central hanging crystal chandelier or period-style wall brackets would be ideal for lighting. Over the mantelpiece, hang a round gilt-framed mirror

Below. *This modern living room has a flavour of Federal America, reflecting Adam's Neo-Classical ideas, with its elegant furniture and arched windows.*

giving a concave reflection—these were highly popular at the time and are easy to obtain in reproduction form. A polished wooden floor with a tapestry type rug make the final touches.

In the bedroom

A simple Colonial-style bedroom is another effective idea to try. Make the walls plain white with the fireplace wall panelled. For added effect make an open fireplace, similar to the one suggested for the Colonial-style dining room. Choose a simple four-poster bed hung with flowered cotton drapes and matching curtains at the windows.

A Dutch painted *kast* or large wardrobe would make another main piece of furniture. It would be fun to try and copy the Dutch-style paintings of the era on a large wardrobe yourself. Use a plain small oak table for a dressing table and upright wooden chairs. Simple Chinese vases would be ideal as decoration, and a patch-work bedspread would look lovely on the bed.

As a complete contrast, think about a Federal-style bedroom, with elegant Sheraton-style furniture. Paint the walls white, with the fireplace, cornice, ceiling and woodwork pale grey. Although fitted carpets were not used at that time, choose a period-style carpet for comfort.

Choose gold and white Regency-style fabric for the bed, upholstery and curtains. A period-style four-poster bed would be ideal, with gold coloured hangings and a plain white satin bedspread, edged with a fringe. Use a plain mahogany dressing table with a wall mirror behind it. On the walls, fix gilt candle-style lights with glass shades, and period-style prints or paintings.

In the living room

Federal fashions were smart, so if you decorate your living room in this style you will bring a fresh elegance to your home. It will be easy to get the effect if you choose rich-looking fabrics in patterns that were popular during the Federal era. Blend these with period-style furniture and wall coverings that are typical of the period and the transformation will be made. An ideal choice would be deep crimson-covered seating and curtains with white paint-work and Chinese-style wallpaper. Add a period-style crystal chandelier, reproduction pictures and china ornaments, and you're there.

Greek styling was popular during the Federal period, when a chaise longue was an important piece of furniture. This would be a must in any living room with a flavour of the period, and it would not look out of place if the rest of the seating is in the form of richly cushioned modern armchairs or a sofa. In fact, half the fun of creating a room is being able to blend the old with the new in an effective way.

An alternative decoration idea would be to paint the walls plain in a rich colour like terracotta, then use a deep classical-style frieze paper round the top of the walls. A wreath pattern or a Greek key design would be ideal for this. Use a narrow frieze paper to make the effect of panels on the walls. Choose Regency stripes for the upholstery and richly draped floor-length curtains of moiré, decorated with fringes and braid, with a swathed pelmet.

TRANSWORLD/AMERICAN HOME

The period touch— Victorian styles and the nineteenth century

The 19th century was a very important era as far as interior design was concerned, because many marked changes were made during this time. This chapter describes the styles popular in the home during Victorian days.

The early 19th century saw the popularity of elegant Regency and Empire designs. Rooms were colourful and smart, making this era one of the most sophisticated as far as room design and furniture were concerned.

After Queen Victoria came to the throne in England, and the economy began to expand quickly on both sides of the Atlantic with the growth of the Industrial Revolution, fashionable home ideas changed dramatically over the world. The 19th century saw the start of machine-made furniture, so cheaper tables, chairs etc were produced, making them available to many more people.

The Classical Greek style that inspired Regency designs still continued to be popular in the 1830s and 40s, but the style was translated more heavily. Furniture was gradually becoming more clumpy and less elegant than beforehand.

By far the most popular furnishing idea that developed during the century was the vogue for furnishings and interiors that reflected past eras. In England, the Gothic era was used as the inspiration for design, while Rococo styles inspired furnishing fashions in America.

The early Victorian styles

Elizabethan styles were popular at this time, and many homes were built to look like small castles or Elizabethan manor houses. Walter Scott's novels, with their historical settings, were great favourites, and these gave rise to what is known as the 'Scottish Baronial' style, when rooms were furnished with heavily carved Elizabethan and Jacobean-type furniture.

Above. *A good example of a Victorian living room, with its mixture of furniture and collection of paintings and knick-knacks. The fringed tablecloth conceals the table legs.*

Louis XIV Rococo styles were also popular. Nearly all furniture made in these styles tended to be on a fairly large scale, with elaborate ornamentation in the form of carving.

Comfort and opulence were considered to be all-important. Chairs with heavily padded seats were found in most homes, and furniture became more rounded, less angular and less leggy. Easy chairs and sofas had deep comfortably padded seats and short legs. What-nots were popular for use as occasional tables or as a display point for ornaments. These can still be found in antique shops.

Papier mâché furniture was also invented during Victorian days and was popular from about the 1830s onwards. It was of delicate construction and light design, contrasting with the more ornate mahogany and oak Gothic and Elizabethan-style furniture.

Papier mâché furniture usually had a black lacquer finish. It was decorated with attractive printed flower designs, inlaid with mother-of-pearl or metals and finished with a dusting of gold or silver. Typical papier mâché furniture included pretty chairs with cane seats, dainty occasional tables and small settees.

Glass conservatories made attractive extensions to many homes, where they were used as a place to show off collections of delicate plants.

Above. This dining room, with its crimson wallpaper, brass picture rails and large, heavily carved sideboard, is typical of the nineteenth century. The Neo-Classical marble mantelpiece with its unusual oval grate of chased brass is a handsome feature.

The open grate went out in favour of fitted grates of cast iron with brass ornamentation. The mantelpiece was large so as to give plenty of space for showing off ornaments. Rooms were close carpeted for extra comfort.

Plate glass was invented during this period, and it made large window panes fashionable instead of the small ones of the Georgian era. Rooms were attractive, with long patterned silk or muslin curtains and flower-patterned or flock wallpapers. Chintz fabrics were used in bedrooms and for loose covers. Semi-transparent blinds were often used at windows. Heavy fabrics like velvet and worsted damask began to gain popularity, but it was not until the mid-Victorian era that they really took over.

Curtains were usually attached to brass or wooden rings and hung from brass or wooden poles. There would be a shallow pleated valance, giving a pelmet effect, hung inside or outside the curtains, and the whole lot was topped by an attractively carved wooden cornice. Fringes, borders and tassels used increasingly as extra decoration. Fabric patterns became bolder, with large flowers and leaves making strong patterns against a plain background. Stripes were also popular, and chairs were sometimes covered in striped satin.

A.W.N. Pugin

During the early Victorian era, the most famous exponent of the Gothic and Elizabethan styles was Pugin, an architect and furniture designer who helped Charles Barry draw up designs for the Houses of Parliament. Pugin did most of the interior design for the Houses of Parliament also, and his ideas had a great influence on house styles in later Victorian days, when rooms were often decorated with richly patterned wallpapers in deep, pompous colours, heavy curtains and hangings and an abundance of ornamentation.

The Great Exhibitions

During the middle part of the nineteenth century, several European countries held large-scale exhibitions which were used as a shop-front for home ideas. Much of the furniture exhibited was almost over-designed. Vast pieces were displayed—monumental sideboards decorated with crowded carving; heavily ornamented wardrobes, cabinets and side tables. These were designed on an almost outlandish scale so that they would catch the eye. Ideas on show in the exhibitions had a great influence on furnishing styles in people's homes and helped to promote the vogue for large furniture and heavily ornamented rooms.

Gimmicky furnishing ideas were also popular and some unusual disguise or 'trompe l'œil' furniture was produced, where materials were given different finishes. Slate was painted and enamelled to look like wood, and woodgrains and inlays were painted on to furniture. Most of this type of furniture was used to make talking-points at the large exhibitions.

Mid-century ideas

This was the worst part of the 19th century. Rooms were dark and dusty from coal fires, they were decorated in depressing colours and crowded with badly assorted collections of small objects. Walls were smothered in pictures from dado to picture rail, and ornaments, especially china ones, were crammed on to shelves and into fashionable display cabinets. Arrangements of shells or dried flowers or stuffed animals or birds were shown off under glass domes. No living room was complete without a large aspidistra in a pot.

The Victorians were prudish in the extreme—they believed that legs should not be seen, and this included not only human legs, but chair, table and piano legs as well. Consequently everything had skirts. Pianos and tables were covered with heavy full-length cloths that discreetly hid their legs. Chairs had loose covers or deep fringes to mask their legs.

Rooms were crammed with furniture to make them look opulent, and a huge sideboard in the dining room was considered a must. They were decorated in drab colours—horrible mixtures of chocolate brown and cream paint, or with heavy floral-patterned wallpapers. Velvet was the most popular furnishing material, either in sombre green or dark red.

A whole collection of different patterns and colours all together in one room was popular. The wallpaper would be one pattern, the curtains another, carpet a third, chair covers yet another, and so on, usually without regard for a dominant colour theme. Chenille cloths were used on tables, and even hearths were decorated with curtains or pelmets. Gilt clocks in glass domes were a popular mantelpiece decoration, and an enormous mirror over the mantelpiece was also considered to be fashionable.

Needlework was a favourite hobby, so hand-embroidered table cloths, carpets and samplers were to be seen in most homes. Much of this work was extremely fine and is now highly prized by collectors.

Heavy velvet curtains let as little light as possible into rooms and cotton lace curtains—thickly patterned—were also hung at the windows to give rooms privacy during the daytime. These tended to keep out yet more light.

Bedrooms were much less over-powering in design, and a Victorian bedroom would be attractive and feminine. Beds, often with half testers, were hung with beautiful flowered chintzes and covered with patchwork quilts. Dressing tables were covered with frilled muslin skirts and other bedroom furniture was of a fairly plain design—making a great contrast to the heavily ornamented pieces used in the rest of the house. Brass beds became extremely

Above. This dining room is in the Gothic revival style, so popular in Victorian homes. Note the arched niche, fitted sideboard, and dark stained chairs with elaborate cresting.
Below. The focal point of this Victorian bedroom is the four-poster bed with muslin drapes. The papier mâché chairs are typical.

fashionable, although the four-poster still continued to be popular. Plain mahogany chests of drawers and wardrobes were used to store clothes.

Aniline dyes were introduced during this period, and this gave much brighter colours to textiles than previously. It also brought about what, to the modern eye, were some horrific colour combinations.

Rooms in towns were usually lit by gas lamps in the form of a central chandelier hanging from the centre of the ceiling, or bracket lights on either side of the chimney piece. Oil lamps were also used.

William Morris

This famous designer's wallpapers and fabrics are, if anything, more popular today than when he designed them a century ago. Morris criticized the impractical and cluttered Victorian homes and called for a return to true decorative arts. So he made furniture, often decorated with paintings by famous artists. Pottery and tiles were also designed.

This was the 'Arts and Crafts Movement', and many well-known designers and artists joined with Morris in his campaign. It was a complete contrast to the popular furnishing ideas of the era and was the origin of the Art Nouveau style, described in greater detail in a later chapter. Morris tried to produce inexpensive furniture that was designed better and on more simple lines than other elaborately decorated mass-produced furniture of the time. He made attractive and simple chairs with rush seats, and cheap furniture that was made cheerful with a green wood stain finish.

William Morris was one of the few people who carried on the old idea of one man designing both the exterior and interior of a home. Usually an architect would design the exterior of a house and the owner's wife would supervize the furnishings. In those days there was less helpful advice available in the form of the abundance of magazine articles and books in interiors than there is today.

Other influence

Another popular designer was Charles Eastlake. His furniture was much more square than the fashionable Victorian curves, and he did much to popularize the use of encaustic tiles for floors and walls up to dado level. These were coloured by burning in paint in brick red, black and white and were usually laid in geometric patterns. He also designed Japanese Gothic-style furniture for mass production.

Transatlantic ideas

Many nineteenth-century American designs were influenced by the Classical designs of Ancient Greece and Rome, rather than by the Gothic fashions that were so popular in Europe. However, Renaissance fashions were popular on both sides of the Atlantic and furnishing fashions travelled more quickly in the 19th century than before. The end of the century saw the beginning of the great American love of antique collecting. European antiques became popular, and French furniture and porcelain in particular were highly prized.

Cottage styles were popular in America, where the old American Colonial and Mission styles were also fashionable.

Late Victorian ideas

Homes were still inspired by earlier historical styles, and one of the favourite fashions was for 'Free Renaissance' designs to conjure up a feeling of the grandeur of Ancient Rome. Furniture was still on a massive scale and inlaid work became popular. Rooms became less drab as more gaudy colours like bright blue and yellow were used together. Plush was a popular fabric, used as long table cloths or as a cover for the mantelpiece. Rich fitted carpets lost popularity and rooms usually had bare board floors with a large mat in the centre or several smaller ones arranged on them.

Japanese-inspired styles became popular and helped to make rooms look lighter and more attractive. Fewer pictures and fewer ornaments were used, and furniture was not so heavily constructed. Gradually homes brightened up, and walls with panelled dados painted white were popular. Above the dado, the walls were often decorated with Japanese-style wall-papers, then there would be a deep frieze paper round the top of the walls.

The 'bracket and overmantel' style was popular for some time. This was a combination of mirrors, small shelves and niches, designed as a tall, single piece to decorate a room above the mantelpiece or sideboard. Palms in pots were the favourite house plants, and were usually placed on tall stands. Lamps were also on tall stands with large frilled shades, and at the end of the century electric light was introduced.

Many of the 19th century ideas for furnishings

*Above. This late Victorian bedroom is made distinctive by the suite of rattan furniture. The wallpaper and curtain fabric are to a design by William Morris. **Below.** A small living room with many details characteristic of the mid-nineteenth century. Note the reading chair with swivel bookrest, patchwork tablecloth and embroidered firescreen. Heavy velvet curtains hang at the windows.*

were overpowering, but there were also some good things that can be used well in modern homes. The next chapter tells you how to get the best from Victorian furnishing ideas. You don't have to produce a dim and religious atmosphere, made depressing by too many bottle green draperies. Get the right touch and you will be able to use these ideas to create added interest in your home.

The period touch— achieving Victorian styles

The photographs and information given in the last chapter should have built up a comprehensive picture of the furnishing styles popular in the 19th century. This chapter goes on to explain how you can interpret those fashions in the context of a modern home, and recreate for yourself a convincing Victorian interior.

Victorian ideas for doing up a home can be adapted well today. You can select the best of the decorations and furniture of the 19th century, knit them together carefully, add a few modern touches, and the result is a sophisticated room scheme.

Some of Victoriana was dreary, but much more of it was attractive, so there are plenty of different ideas and furnishings to whet the appetite.

Rooms decorated in several different patterns and colours were popular. This kind of effect is difficult to achieve successfully and not necessarily all that pleasing, because rooms decorated with several different patterns and colours often tend to look a complete jumble. The modern translation of this idea is to decorate a room with several different patterns, but all based on one single colour theme.

Try this idea for a living room, taking milk chocolate brown as the dominant colour. Start with a brown geometrically patterned carpet. Choose chocolate coloured paint for the walls, topped with a frieze paper, or a brown leafy or sculptural-patterned wallpaper. Add plain white or beige curtains, patterned with a wide brown border, or choose a curtain fabric to match the wallpaper. Choose loose covers in a brown fabric with a small pattern; in a striped fabric that keeps to the brown theme; or in a plain beige, white or chocolate brown with the skirts patterned, using the same border for this as for the curtains.

Now add lots of cushions in as many different brown-patterned fabrics as you can collect from the remnant counter in your nearest furniture store. Cover round occasional tables with long patchwork or plain cloths, keeping to the brown theme, and add popular 19th century knick-knacks in the form of stuffed birds or artificial flowers under a glass dome, old oil lamps and an aspidistra in a large pot.

There is no need to crowd a room with furniture as it would have been in the 19th century— you can still add a feeling of the era by using a few typical furnishings, draperies and accessories.

One or two pieces of Victorian furniture, like an elaborate mahogany-framed chaise longue or a button back chair, contrast well with ultra-modern furniture and go a long way towards softening the whole look of what could otherwise be a stark room scheme.

Creating a 19th century atmosphere is fun, and luckily plenty of hand-me-downs from that era are still to be found. Victorian ornaments and furniture, however, are rapidly gaining in popularity with antique collectors. If you're lucky you can pick out some good bargains in country antique shops or large second-hand furniture marts. The furniture is nearly always a good buy, because it's solidly built, and will not be too complicated to renovate.

Above. *Many characteristic features give this living room a cosy Victorian touch. Note the oil lamp, knick knacks displayed on the mantelpiece, and the closely grouped pictures.*

JOHN BETHELL

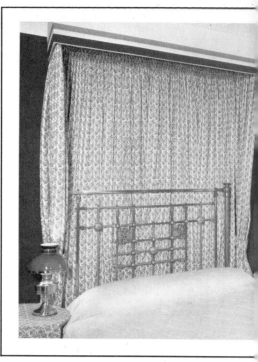

BRIAN MORRIS

Ideas for curtains

One of the best ways of creating the atmosphere of a particular period is by making curtains that echo the fashions of the era. Here are some typical 19th century ideas for curtains. These could be used in either a living room, a dining room, a bedroom or a hall.

Curtains were full length, reaching from the top of the window frame to the floor. They were often topped with elaborately carved wooden pelmets, which can be found in junk shops and are a good buy because they help to create the full 19th century effect.

One not too elaborate design is to have curtains of damask or velvet with heavy cotton lace ones underneath. Pull the curtains almost across the window and catch them into heavy loops, held by silky tasselled cord at the sides. Catch the lace curtains back as well so they make another draped effect inside the velvet ones.

Top the curtains with a carved 'cornice' or pelmet and under this fix a draped 'valance' or pelmet of damask or velvet. Cut a piece of velvet twice as wide as the width of the window and one third as long. Cut the fabric carefully so that when it is hanging, the base of the valance will be gently arched over the centre and fall into a deep curve and a point at each side.

The easiest way to do this is to fold the fabric in half and draw the shape on with tailor's chalk —in this way both sides will be equal. Now fold the valance into box pleats. There should be about a 2in. to 3in. gap between each fold, which should fall in a soft drape rather than a pressed knife pleat. Edge the base of the valance with a deep fringe and finish the points on either side with large tassels.

Another idea is to use plain deep red or green velvet for generously gathered curtains in an 'Elizabethan' style. Edge the curtains on the inside and bottom with an elaborate border. Hang the curtains from a wooden pole. Top the window with a carved pelmet, and behind the curtains hang an ungathered valance cut in a castellated or deeply scalloped shape. Edge the valance with braid and attach a long tassel to the base of each scallop. Interface the valance with buckram or a stiff interlining.

Try heavy damask or brocatelle curtains, edged with braid and looped to either side of the window. Underneath hang a wide lace curtain, caught into a deep loop across to one side of the window only. Add a draped valance and wooden pelmet and decorate the valance with plenty of braid and tassels.

Alternatively try rich velvet curtains, edged with braid. Underneath these put muslin curtains, edged with a border. Top the curtains with a wooden pelmet and a muslin valance, hanging over the front of the curtains in festoons or deeply scalloped horizontal gathers.

On a much more simple scale, flower-patterned curtains, edged with a plain braid, looped to the sides of the window and hung on a heavy pole with brass rings would still give a good Victorian effect, especially if you use tassels on the curtain loops. Line and interline the curtains so they hang well.

Choose a rich heavy fabric for a living or dining room window and a lighter flower-patterned chintz for a bedroom.

Above. *The chocolate brown walls, half tester bed, oil lamps and papier mâché chair all combine to give this modern bedroom a delicate and feminine Victorian feeling.*
Right. *A richer and grander example of a Victorian-style bedroom, with deep crimson carpet and chair covers, chintz curtains and drapes, and a heavy wooden four-poster bed.*

In the living room

Early 19th century interior fashions were colourful and attractive, and here is an idea for a living room. Start with a fitted carpet in a floral or fleur-de-lys pattern. Add wallpaper with a delicate floral pattern on a pastel or white background, and pastel or white woodwork. Good wallpaper shops carry ranges of old wallpaper designs which are reproductions of originals, and you should be able to get help from the salesmen in choosing an appropriate pattern. Look for papers patterned with roses, leaves, or flowers and birds.

Choose long curtains in a plain silky fabric with soft diaphanous muslin ones underneath. Cover chairs in silky-type fabrics—Regency stripes were highly popular in the early 19th century. Choose clear colours for the furnishings that tone with the wallpaper and curtains. Good colours to choose would be bright yellow, clear green, turquoise or scarlet. Use one of these as the main colour for the curtains and pick it out in the pattern of the chair covers and carpet.

Furniture at this time would have been made of rosewood, and reproduction furniture in this attractive wood can now be found. If you're lucky enough to have an old piece of papier mâché furniture, add this to underline the period feeling. If your living room has two long windows at one end of the room, hang a tall gilt-framed mirror or pier glass in between the windows, with a rosewood occasional table underneath. Add another gilt-framed mirror above the mantelpiece—this would have been marble or white-painted wood.

On the mantelpiece place an elaborate gilt clock in a glass dome, and Chinese-style vases or china ornaments on either side. Other small accessories that would look attractive would be a fire screen, a needlework box and a small rosewood writing table. Choose watercolour pictures in gold frames for the walls, brass fireguard and firearms, and period-style lighting. Nineteenth century oil lamps and brass candelabra with glass shades are popular home accessories in most parts of the world. Although original ones are fairly expensive, modern reproduction oil lamps which have been converted to take electric bulbs are easy to find in the shops.

Later 19th century fashions became heavier, with mahogany furniture and velvet hangings being the great favourites. A living room would have an elaborate fireplace, topped with mirrors and shelves. This type of 'overmantel' can often be found cheaply in junk shops and is fun to renovate. It makes a good feature in a modern or period style room. Paint the wooden frame and shelves white to give a lighter effect, or leave the dark polished wood as it is, if you want a truer Victorian atmosphere.

Cover the mantelpiece with a fitted cloth in brocatelle or velvet and add a deep and elaborately designed fringe round the edge. Search the junk shops for inexpensive Victorian tiles for the fireplace, which should have a black cast iron fitted grate, and a brass fender, coal scuttle etc. On the shelves of the overmantel, place an assortment of period-style ornaments—china figures, elaborately patterned jugs etc. On either side of the fireplace, hang old miniatures or silhouette pictures.

Pictures crowded on the walls were popular in the 19th century. There is no need to clutter all the walls of a room with pictures in the same way as the Victorians did, but you can get the feeling well in a living room by treating just one wall as a Victorian picture gallery. This works especially well in a room that is mainly furnished with modern things.

A mass of pictures helps to make a room seem fuller and more interesting. Either choose an assortment of similar pictures (perhaps by the same artist) in matching frames, or use a collection of different pictures and frames—some watercolours, some etchings etc. Add two or three Victorian-style china plates and even a small mirror in a gilt frame. Draw an imaginary frame on the wall to mark the edges of the picture gallery and arrange the pictures and plates attractively within this frame. Use your material with care and the effect will be both interesting and attractive.

A typically Victorian arrangement of furniture for an opulent mid-century living room is to have a desk facing the window with easy chairs and a settee or chaise longue ranged round the fire in an asymmetrical group. Each chair could have a small occasional table beside it. Add an inexpensive basket chair with large cushioned seat—these were great favourites and are still made in the same traditional design today.

Choose loose covers of chintz for the chairs; cover the tables with long fringed cloths and choose curtains with a large pattern. Add a straight gathered pelmet, its edges decorated with a plain border. Instead of muslin undercurtains, use plain white or cream holland blinds. As extra furnishings, scout round junk shops for a what-not and a display cabinet to house a collection of Victorian ornaments. Add a large aspidistra in a pot as the final touch.

Try making an American-style 19th century corner in the living room, as this would add character to the room without overpowering it. Search round junk shops for an old carved oak press cupboard and on this place a collection of popular ornaments and accessories of the era. Choose things like an oil lamp, an old photograph in a silver frame, china or pottery figurines, an arrangement of artificial flowers under a glass dome and a jug of fresh flowers. Group pictures on the wall round the cupboard—preferably watercolour landscapes in gilt frames. On one side of the cupboard, have a button back chair upholstered in richly coloured velvet and on the other a large palm in an ornate pot.

In the dining room

Dining rooms in the mid and late 19th century were usually decorated in deep, yet rich, colours to give a formal splendour. This effect would be an interesting one to recreate. Although the rich colours are not necessarily practical and tend to be dark, they do look splendid under artificial light for a party. So if you do a lot of formal entertaining, this rich-looking room would be an ideal one to make.

Select a richly patterned wallpaper with a Gothic design in crimson, deep green, purple or royal blue with gold. Alternatively, choose a period style flock wallpaper. Curtains should be

Above. A Victorian corner in a modern dining room. The fireplace is typical, with its padded fender seat, glass domed clock and candlesticks. Note the ornate coal scuttle.

HEIDEDE CARSTENSEN

richly draped with tassels, braid etc and made from velvet or a heavy damask-type fabric. Choose mahogany furniture—balloon back dining chairs were popular in the 19th century and these can be found today. Upholster the seats in striped satin, buttoned leather, velvet or tapestry.

Circular mahogany dining tables were sometimes used in small rooms, or long carved tables of oak or mahogany, so either of these styles would be suitable. The more massive the sideboard the better, and the more carving it is covered with the better. If your dining room is small, try to suit the scale of the furniture to the size of the room, with the large sideboard as the dominant feature. Decorate the sideboard with Victorian knick-knacks—glass or wax fruit in a bowl, glass vases decorated with lustres, a clock, elaborately worked pewter teapot and jug, or glass decanters.

Cover the table with a large cloth in chenille or a rich-looking fabric. For a round table, choose a circular floor-length cloth, edged with an opulent border and a fringe. If you make the cloth, there are many attractive fabrics on the market. Complete the picture with 19th. century style china and glass. This is popular at the moment, so reasonably inexpensive reproductions of favourite 19th century china designs like the famous willow pattern can be found easily in Britain and the United States.

In the bedroom

A bedroom in the 19th century was often the most attractive room in the house. Colours would be lighter than in downstairs rooms and the effect much more colourful and pleasing to the eye. French-style bedrooms were particularly feminine and luxurious, and a bedroom of this type would be a good one to recreate.

Start with the bed in an alcove, and choose draped pelmets of silky fabric, patterned or plain, to frame the whole of the bed alcove.

Make a matching pelmet for the main windows of the room with curtains of silk, then make curtains for the bed alcove, and matching ones to go behind the silk curtains at the window. For these you could use a figured muslin or lace edged with a border and fringe and looped at the sides. Choose a mahogany bed to go in the alcove and cover it with a muslin or lace bedspread, edged with a deep fringe. To complete the effect, make a lace canopy for the bed, hanging over the head and the foot of the bed, then draped up and caught in a pelmet to give a crown effect in the centre top of the alcove above the bed.

Use a softly flower-patterned wallpaper, then add a frieze to match the curtain border. This border can also be used on the chairs. Add a draped dressing table, using muslin or lace to match the bed hangings. Choose a crystal light fitting, and cover the floor with a fitted carpet. Arrange plenty of pictures on the walls. If there's room, put a day bed or chaise longue by the window, then add large pot plants and Victorian-style accessories.

On a less elaborate scale, choose a flowery wallpaper and chintz curtains and covers for the bed. Choose a brass bed or an old-style carved mahogany or oak one with a half tester, which can be decorated with a plain or frilled valance to match the bed hangings. Complete the effect with a patchwork bedspread. Choose a fitted carpet in a period-style pattern. A marble-topped wash stand would be another good piece of furniture to choose, and small round bedside tables covered with tartan or patchwork cloths. Make large cushions with frilled edges to decorate the bed and easy chairs, which can be covered with loose covers of chintz fabric.

These ideas should help you bring a 19th century feeling into your home without going to unreasonable expense.

BILL McLAUGHLIN

The period touch— the 1920s and 1930s look

Interior styles in the 19th century became very ornate and cluttered, and it is not surprising that there was a marked reaction against them. This chapter describes the simpler fashions that followed the crowded Victorian interiors, detailing in particular *art nouveau* and *art deco* designs. It goes on to explain ways of re-creating the look of the 1920s and 1930s in a modern home.

Above. A cool living/dining room with clean art nouveau-inspired lines. The characteristic chrome furniture and mirror tiles complement the black and white colour scheme.

The craze for *art nouveau* designs in Britain, Europe and America at the end of the 19th century and the beginning of the 20th developed almost directly from William Morris and the British Arts and Crafts Movement. Morris's quest for beauty in design was a reaction against ugly industrialized products. He did much to revive good craftsmanship in the late 19th century and brought craftsmen in different fields together for an exchange of ideas. Much of Morris's work was influenced by the Pre-Raphaelites—a group of artists, including Dante Gabriel Rossetti. The artists, together

Above. An attractive art nouveau corner, with some striking details. Note the silver mirror frame, sculptural lamp holder and potted plants. Left. A Tiffany-style lamp with glass sections casts a gentle glow over this art nouveau scene, with its screen and ornate carved and gilded wooden table base, set against the William Morris wallpaper.

with Morris and other notable craftsmen, produced beautifully made furniture, often decorated with painted panels or with tiles.

Furniture designed by Morris and other followers of the Arts and Crafts Movement was much more practical and generally better proportioned than the heavy ornate furniture that was so widely popular at the time. The Arts and Crafts Movement members disliked the highly cluttered Victorian rooms, and the homes they designed tended to be decorated on more simple lines.

Textiles and wallpapers, particularly by A. H. Mackmurdo, started to be made in *art nouveau* patterns. They were decorated with winding stalks, leaves and curving floral patterns.

Charles Rennie Mackintosh, a Scottish

designer who worked mainly in Glasgow, was another famous exponent of the *art nouveau* style. The houses he designed had simple and uncluttered interiors, while the furniture, with strange tall-backed chairs, was prophetically modern in appearance. Mackintosh often used white enamelled finishes on woodwork, and his designs particularly heralded today's stark furniture.

Another famous craftsman and designer was a Belgian, Victor Horta. In the 1890s, he designed a house for a family called Tassel in Brussels. He made great use of curved floral motifs and flowers and this house did much to popularize the use of *art nouveau* after it had been featured in design and fashion magazines.

Louis Comfort Tiffany

Stained glass lampshades designed by Tiffany, an American, are the epitome of *art nouveau*. These lampshades were popular at the turn of the century, when people used them hung low over dining tables. Lamps in the Tiffany style have recently become popular again.

The almost fussy *art nouveau* designs, with differently coloured pieces of glass in the

shades, contrast well with simple modern interiors. An original Tiffany shade is now something of a treasure for collectors, but reproduction ones can be found in major lighting shops and in good department stores.

Art Nouveau and its successors

Aubrey Beardsley and Toulouse Lautrec are two artists whose work is also typical of the *art nouveau* style, as well as the other designers already mentioned.

The fashion for *art nouveau* did not last long, although it was a great influence on the decorative arts for some years. There was a sudden vogue for classical designs just before the First World War. Antique furniture gained popularity, particularly in Britain and America. Expert craftsmen would fake old furniture so as to make more available to the public.

At the same time as all this, the modern movement was taking shape in Britain, America and on the Continent. Frank Lloyd Wright, a famous American architect, designed cube-shaped chairs—a total contrast to the leafy *art nouveau* styles. He believed that furniture should blend with the architecture of a house, rather than contrast with it.

The Bauhaus and the 1920s style

On the Continent, designers began to produce less ornamented furniture and architectural styles; they aimed for simplicity. After the First World War, a new design school called the Bauhaus was started in Dessau, Germany. Students were encouraged to experiment with modern materials in their designs. The accent of the school was on the future, rather than concentrating on studies of the past as most art and design schools did. At the Bauhaus the first cantilevered chairs and furniture designs using tubular steel were produced.

The school indirectly revolutionized the thinking of architects and designers. When it was closed down by the Nazis in 1933, many of its teachers moved to other parts of the world, particularly America, where they continued their work and were a great influence on architecture and furniture design.

During the 1920s one of the most famous architects of the century, a Frenchman called Le Corbusier, said:"A house is a machine for living in". This was one of the main themes for house design and furnishing of the era.

Many 1920s and Bauhaus designs were based on shapes like the cube, the circle and the rectangle. Furnishings were cut down to a minimum and designs were functional and uncluttered. The Bauhaus did much to promote good design in the furniture industry.

White paint on the walls was by far the most popular method of room decoration, especially in France where Le Corbusier was saying that white paint on the walls expressed cleanliness and efficiency. After that famous dictum wallpapers became less fashionable, and those that were popular tended to be in geometric or small floral patterns, often in colours like silver, black, white and grey.

Metal tubing was one of the most common materials used for furniture design, and lacquered furniture was also popular. Woods such as rosewood, sycamore and oak were widely used, because the beautiful wood grain made a natural decoration on a starkly functional piece of furniture. Many designers worked towards producing low-cost but stylish furniture for mass production.

The 1920s were also the days of avant garde artistic movements. Much of the decoration reflected these movements. Cubism influenced the design of square chunky furniture. Futurism brought a feeling of speed and energy, particularly to fabric designs with 'free-form' patterns in clear colours—a great contrast to the more realistic patterns of earlier days.

Art Deco and the 1930s style

People's homes became less austere in the 1930s. After the obsession for functional things in the 1920s, rooms became more elegant. At the start of the decade rooms were still fairly plain and simply furnished, often because young couples were working to a tight budget as a result of the depression at the end of the 1920s.

Wallpapers were still out of fashion, and beautiful murals were used instead to decorate walls. Rex Whistler was one of the most famous British artists who decorated rooms in this way. Curtains and carpets took on a new look, patterned with swirling abstract designs or geometric styles.

This was the era of *art deco*. The name is short for *Exposition des Arts Décoratifs et Industriels*, a famous exhibition held in Paris in 1925. This exhibition influenced design greatly towards the end of the 1920s and during the 1930s. It took time for housing fashions to permeate through to everyday life from the high priests of *art deco* and style setters in the form of avant garde architects and designers with rich patrons who encouraged their work.

Art deco styles were linear, with geometric patterns, circles and ovals. Colours were bright —emerald green, violet, orange and deep blue. Designs were more controlled than in the *art nouveau* era, and the most popular *art deco* motifs can be seen not only on furniture and textiles, but also on pottery and glass as well as on doors and house fronts.

Built-in furniture became popular, making rooms much less cluttered. Surrealist ideas were fashionable, and one of the most famous examples is a lamp, made from a pair of china hands, holding a globular shade. Lighting became an art and decorators tried to design rooms with indirect or concealed lighting. Shiny satin was one of the most popular fabrics; it was used particularly for curtains and lampshades.

Furniture was 'modern' looking, made from glass, chrome and steel. Great use was made of mirrors, particularly in alcoves and bathrooms, and walls were often covered with grainy wood veneers. Star patterns on fabrics were popular, and rubber plants and potted palms were widely used for extra decoration.

While many decorators were mixing 'modern' furniture and creating *art deco* ideas for smart and elegant room settings, others mixed the new with the old in an effective way, particularly in England and the United States. This second style became known as the International style and has changed little since the 1930s.

In Britain and the United States there was a deep feeling for historical styles and antiques.

TIM STREET PORTER/ELIZABETH WHITING

Above. *This eye-catching living room is decorated in the art deco style. Typical features are the Egyptian-style tables, angular wall brackets and standard lamp, and black cubist-style table and ornaments.*
Right. *A spectacular collection of art deco knick knacks. Note the beads, vases, sequinned collar and marble book ends.*

BILL McLAUGHLIN

Much reproduction furniture was made in Tudor, Sheraton, Queen Anne and other styles. In Britain 'mock Tudor' was one of the most popular architectural styles and it can now be seen in many rows of houses all over the country.

Achieving the period touch

Creating *art nouveau* or 1920s and 1930s style rooms can be fun. The best thing about early 20th century style interiors is that the actual accessories and furniture can still be found in second-hand shops and junk furnishing stores at reasonable prices. So getting the period touch can be a good exercise in low-budget home-making. All you need is a good spotter's eye, and you will recognize the right-looking bargain when you see it.

In the living room

One of the most simple ideas of the 1930s and one of the most striking ones to create is to make a one-colour living room. The interior designer Syrie Maugham created a famous all-white living room in 1933. It was one of the most well-known rooms of the decade and her ideas were copied by many people in their own homes.

Rather than choosing a totally white theme, select cream, ivory or off-white, so the room will not look too cold. Paint all the walls and woodwork in the chosen colour. Either paint the floorboards white or choose white tiles or sheet vinyl, covered with a large plain white mat. Look for two low and comfortably cushioned sofas to arrange opposite each other. Cover these in beige satin, or choose a pale, yet shiny fabric like cotton satin that will give the effect less expensively. The covers should be plain without skirts and should be edged with a white fringe.

Add simply styled occasional tables, painted to match the woodwork, and choose white curtains to match the sofas. Look for white 1930s style accessories from junk shops— pottery figurines etc—and add an arrangement of dried flowers in a plain glass vase. As a

BILL McLAUGHLIN

JOHN BETHELL

Left. *A 1920s style living room, with William Morris wallpaper and display of art nouveau objects.* **Above.** *This house, built in 1937, is an important example of the International Modern Movement. Note the iron frame windows and chrome chairs.*

special feature, cover an alcove wall with mirror tiles. Make table lamps from plain white pottery vases, finished with stiff white parchment shades, or look for actual 1930s type lights.

Wallpaper and fabric designs of the *art nouveau* era are fairly easy to obtain now, and these will be the best help when you make an *art nouveau* style living room. Cover your existing furnishings with *art nouveau* style fabrics. Look for a tall *art nouveau* style flower pot on a stand and in it place a shiny leafed house plant. Search round for small items of real *art nouveau* furniture like bamboo tables.

Curtains could be either in chintz to match the wallpaper, or in a plain woven fabric with an *art nouveau* patterned border. The curtains should be hung on a plain wooden rail. Add Tiffany-style lampshades hung low over occasional tables, or used on a table lamp. For the floor, sand and seal the floorboards and cover them with patterned rugs. Plain large rugs with leafy borders were popular and these can sometimes be found cheaply in second-hand furniture shops. As wall decorations use reproduction posters by Toulouse Lautrec or Aubrey Beardsley. These can be found in most good poster shops.

In the dining room

For an *art nouveau* dining room, again choose the subtly coloured leafy swirling designs for wallpaper and fabrics that echo that particular era. Alternatively, paint the walls in a plain colour to match a deep frieze paper round the top of the walls and round the room immediately above the skirting board. Furnishings should be simple; rush-seated or bentwood dining chairs with an oak gate-leg table and a plain dresser. Over the table hang a Tiffany lampshade on a long flex. Hang willow pattern or country-style

plates on the wall. Add patterned rugs and a floor-length table cloth in swirling *art nouveau* patterns.

For a 1920s or Bauhaus-style dining room, choose a starkly simple black and white colour scheme. Black tubular steel chairs in a canti-lever design, or black cube-style chairs would be best. Choose a simple white round dining table—your own one painted white could give the effect—and a dresser painted white. Paint three walls white and one charcoal grey, and choose a plain grey carpet. Add 1920s style paintings—Piccasso reproduction prints are ideal.

Ideas from the 1930s are excellent for small homes. Built-in furniture saved space and rooms were not overcrowded. Look for a 1930s style table and chairs in a junk shop. Polish up the table to show off the wood grain, or cover the table top with a mirror and paint the legs deep mauve. Cover the dining chairs in white leatherette. Paint the walls mauve, the ceiling white, and add ivory satin curtains and a 1930s style bracket light. If the room is small, remove the fireplace. Keep the floor plain and polished with the addition of a geometrically patterned mat.

In the bedroom

An *art nouveau* bedroom is a simple one to create. Look for a brass bedstead that can be covered with an *art nouveau* style fabric to match the curtains and wallpaper. On either side of the bed, place small round occasional tables covered with circular fringed cloths. Choose simple pottery table lamps topped with lacy shades or Tiffany lights hanging low over the tables. Cover the floor with a large patterned rug.

One of the most famous bedrooms of the 1920s in France was the one designed for

Jeanne Lanvin, the famous couturier. The colour scheme of deep cornflower or 'Lanvin' blue and cream was especially attractive, and the idea would be effective to copy. The whole room was covered with silk, patterned with yellow and white flowers and palms in a fairly regular pattern.

Look for a deep blue wallpaper with a matching fabric to get this effect without the expense of silk. Make a low divan bed in an alcove with cupboards on either side. The cupboards should be covered with wallpaper and have arched doorways, with curtains to match the wallpaper hung inside them, instead of doors. Add a fringed or beaded pelmet, gathered across the top of the alcove, and a fitted bedspread with big cushions, all in the blue fabric.

Add low, buttoned chairs, the woodwork painted pale blue, upholstered in a plain blue silky fabric. Over the bed hang a light covered in a creamy silk shade. For a dressing table, paint a simple table pale blue to match the chairs, or drape it with skirts of the blue fabric.

Bedrooms in the 1930s often had a Holly-wood splendour. They were hung with pale pink satin and decorated with tinted mirrors. A bedroom of this type is certainly luxurious, though the pale colours are not always practical. Choose a buttoned bedhead in white leather or satin, a plain bedspread and curtains also in satin. Add fringed satin cushions, white fur rugs and a dressing table draped in satin. Choose white built-in furniture for everything else to give the final 'Hollywood' touch.

With some of these ideas in mind, you will find it satisfying to copy rooms of this era, and if you own a between-the-wars house you will be able to create a total look for your home.

GRAZIA NERI

Above. This elegant Italian living room is indisputably modern. Typical features include the chrome lights, black acrylic furniture and two-level carpeted seating area.

The period touch— modern design: 1

This series, which details furnishing styles through the ages and shows how to give a period flavour to your home, has now come right up to the present time. This chapter covers the development of modern design, explaining the influence of Scandinavian and Italian trends and also the popularity of country furniture.

Small homes where space is at a premium have brought about a great change in furnishing styles. Old storage furniture, heavy bookcases, wardrobes and chests, all use up valuable floor space, and this has prompted designers to invent streamlined modular furniture to fit along the walls. These neat built-in units help to create a much greater feeling of space in the home.

At the same time, recent inventions like central heating and strip lighting have replaced what were once highly necessary furnishings, like fireplaces or stoves, large oil lamps and hefty candelabra. The built-in unit has become a hold-all, and ornaments that once graced the mantelpiece are displayed on

CLIVE CORLESS

its shelves. Hidden strip lights or spotlights are used instead of cumbersome chandeliers.

Many designers, like the famous American, the late Frank Lloyd Wright, plan a room architecturally, so that everything is built in, including seating in the form of an attractive conversation pit or seating platform. Then there is no need for any free-standing furniture. The focal point of a room is the people in it, rather than the furnishings, which make the backcloth.

Recent discoveries, such as laminated finishes, especially for table tops; dirt-resistant sprays for upholstery fabrics; washable wall-papers that are easy to put up and just as easy to strip off; vinyl floorings; these have all helped to revolutionize the way we decorate our homes. Today's homes are much more functional than the stark 'modern' homes of the 1920s, far more comfortable and full of colour.

One of the best things about the modern touch is that anything goes. Brand-new furniture can be mixed with old in an effective way. In some of the most up-to-date homes featured in the pages of international furnishing magazines, you see rooms furnished with built-in seating and storage units. The walls may have a plain brick finish. There may be a plain fitted carpet and long semi-sheer curtains. The effect is completed by one beautiful old piece of furniture—perhaps a carved table or an antique marquetry cabinet. This old piece of furniture helps to contrast with the uncluttered modern ideas. The built-in seating merges into the background as part of the room, while the carved furniture adds a friendly touch that is often lacking in homes furnished with a totally modern scheme.

The idea of mixing the old with the new is a great help to people with new homes, because it can make furnishing costs far less expensive. You can select what you like and mix it together to make a room that reflects your personality. Furnishing a room in a modern way doesn't mean you have to throw out all the old things, it means you look at them with a fresh

Above. A strikingly up-to-date dining room with an unmistakable Italian flavour. The glass table top and acrylic chairs allow a good view of the geometric patterned carpet.
Below. A less colourful but no less effective dining room. The totally white colour scheme is softened by the light from the candles. The painting completes the modern theme.

eye and do them up in a modern way, using sparkling new finishes and ideas for colour.

If you want a room with both the old and new in it, then your local junk shops should produce all sorts of interesting bits and pieces to inspire you. You can create your own modern-style built-in seating or storage units to save even more money. Window seats are especially space-saving and attractive, particularly in a Georgian bow or bay window. Add something new in the form of an inexpensive blow-up chair, or a giant floor cushion; add something old in the form of your junk shop buy, smartly renovated, and you will have furnished the room at minimum cost. Renovating old furniture is usually quite a simple and enjoyable task and the results can be stunning.

If totally modern furnishings appeal to you, then again it should not be difficult to get the right effect. New manufacturing processes make it possible for the world's best designs to be made cheaply enough for the low-cost market. Before the days of furniture manufacturers, furniture was craftsman-made and usually pricey. Today's furniture is architect- or crafts-man-designed, yet often inexpensive.

There is such a wide choice of finishes and fabrics on the market that it is possible to give an individual look to even the most common mass-produced piece of furniture. A different paint for the framework of a table, an unusual upholstery fabric—these are just two simple ways of making something that is mass-produced change its character to suit your own special ideas for creating a room scheme.

MICHAEL BOYS

The development of modern design

William Morris and his associates in Victorian days took the first steps towards modern design. They were followed in the 1920s and 1930s by Le Corbusier, Marcel Breuer, Frank Lloyd Wright and the Bauhaus School for design (see the previous chapter).

Since those days the aim of designers has been to improve on the originals and to introduce totally new furnishing and decoration ideas. The main aim is still to make homes that are comfortable and functional, furnished with things that are simple to manufacture and attractive to the eye.

America is one of the main countries to have influenced modern styles in the home. Just before the Second World War, the Museum of Modern Art, New York, ran a competition for furniture design. This was won by Charles Eames and Eero Saarinen, who are now two of the best-known names in modern design.

The chair they designed to win the competition was a complete innovation at the time. The seat, back and arms were moulded all in one piece, then covered with a thin layer of rubber for comfort and finished with a smart upholstery fabric. The original legs were aluminium, but wartime shortages meant this metal had to be substituted by wood when the chair went into production. The idea behind the design was to reduce the number of parts necessary in the making up of the chair so that it would be an extremely simple item to manufacture. It was also designed to be comfortable as well as lightweight.

Above. A characteristically stark Scandinavian-style interior, with plain wood floor and ceiling, bold colours, modern pictures and sparse furnishings.
Below. This living room has a cosy country look, making a contrast to the austere appearance of many modern schemes. It nonetheless reflects current trends.

Eames and Saarinen were also responsible for many other famous furniture designs, like chairs of plywood moulded to a comfortable shape to fit the body, pedestal tables and chairs of moulded glassfibre and plastic, and simple storage units to be fixed up in different ways for different purposes. Saarinen designed the famous 'womb' chair in the mid-1940s. This was a deep, comfortable chair of moulded plastic with thick foam upholstery, supported on a metal frame and legs.

Britain has also made an important contribution to the international field of modern design. Clive Latimer and Robin Day have produced good-looking furniture designs, and David Hicks, an internationally famous interior decorator, has created striking geometric designs for carpets and helped to make people more conscious of the art of furnishing a home. The famous furnishing firm of Heals has done much to promote modern designs and create an international exchange of ideas.

The Scandinavian influence

Scandinavia has been one of the greatest influences on modern design in the home. In all the Scandinavian countries there is a great living tradition of craftsmanship. This is one of the main reasons why Scandinavian furnishings are of such a high quality. In Denmark and Finland particularly, furniture is often hand-made by craftsmen in workshops. As modern home design has developed, Scandinavian craftsmen and architects have used their skills to invent fresh ways of making modern furnishings with traditional materials. Teak furniture in sleek 1970s styles, and beautiful folkweave fabrics giving a totally modern approach in design and colouring are two examples of how Scandinavian ideas have made their mark.

As well as the craft workshops, there is also a flourishing furniture manufacturing trade in Scandinavia. Some of the most interesting designs using new materials have come from

two famous Danes, Arne Jacobsen and Hans Wegner. They have produced practical, yet beautiful-looking designs for things like modular storage units and Jacobsen's renowned 'egg' and 'swan' chairs.

From Finland have come some progressive designs for glass, and Marimekko's fabrics have had a great influence on the design of modern fabrics for the home. Their furnishing cottons, for example, are patterned with strong, often sculptural shapes in clear and bright colours. A blind in a Marimekko fabric and a chair by Arne Jacobsen are sure to add an effective modern touch to any room.

The cool professional designs of the Scandinavians with their sleek, uncluttered homes and their love of natural surfaces has had a great impact on house design in all parts of the world. The Scandinavians, especially, like rooms with walls in natural textures like brick and wood. Furnishings are reduced to a minimum. Rooms of this type can be effective to look at and restful, as well as practical to live in.

The Italian influence

It is mainly since World War II that Italian designs and ideas have exploded on to the international furnishing scene. While the Scandinavians have perfected modern designs with traditional materials, the Italian designers like Geo Ponti and Carlo Mollino have gone overboard for using new materials in a wealth of different ways.

Italian designs are streamlined and curvaceous, yet almost light-hearted in their approach. Much of the furniture is expensive, particularly some of the more extraordinary modern chairs, sculptured from foam and covered in materials like shiny pvc. But there is also much that is inexpensive, like sack chairs and beautiful fold-up dining chairs with seats and back rests of clear acrylic with shiny lightweight metal frames.

Italian lighting is worth a special mention. It has helped to turn lighting from what was often considered a dull necessity into an art. At the inexpensive end of the international market there are neatly curved table lights in colourful moulded plastic, and at the pricey end there are strangely shaped hoses with lights inside that look like curled up snakes, chrome table lamps looking almost like spiders, and tall standard lamps on long chrome legs, topped with white globular shades. One of the best known Italian lighting designers is H. Guzzini.

Italian design is, above all, futuristic. Yet some of the ideas that today seem like expensive flights of fancy could well be forerunners of the even more automated living promised for the future. For instance, one of Italy's best-known designers, the late Joe Columbo, furnished an extraordinary apartment in Milan. He removed all the interior walls and divided the space into three areas—living, sleeping and cooking. Huge floor-to-ceiling accordian screens of a silver plastic fabric were electrically operated to separate the areas when necessary.

At one end of the apartment was a 'closing-bed'. Its large headboard was fitted with a host of electronic devices, from built-in cigarette lighters to air conditioning controls. The bed could be entirely covered with a huge yellow plastic canopy that was folded down electronically from the tall chrome-covered headboard. It worked like a pram hood, and when it was down the sleeper was kept fully air-conditioned inside! At the other end of the room was an invention called 'Rotoliving'. This was a large built-in electronic unit which combined a dining table, seating area and bar, and incorporated a television and stereo built into a revolving central core which was made of laminated plastic. Perhaps this apartment was an example of a totally 'built-in' living to come in the future.

Italy also has a great craft tradition, and just one way in which they are putting a new face on traditional products is with ceramic tiles, which are exported all over the world. These come in a huge range of clear and precise designs that feature geometric, floral or sculptural patterns in bright or subtle colours.

Other trends

With fashions travelling all over the world so quickly, new and inexpensive home ideas soon catch on. Blow-up chairs are a typical example of this. These can be found in America, Europe and Australia. Knock-down and toughened cardboard furniture is a speciality of British designers and this, too, has become fashionable in many parts of the world because it is an ideal choice for people decorating on a low budget. Inexpensive French earthenware pottery and cooking utensils are also popular international favourites. Huge floor cushions, oriental paper lampshades—these can all be

Below. This dining hall is a good example of the combination of old and new styles. The design scheme is very modern, but the antique furniture blends in well.

MICHAEL BOYS

used in many different ways to give personality to your home.

The final popular furnishing trend today is for rooms with a country atmosphere. In recent years, particularly, the demand for the fresh country look has become almost as great as the demand for modern furniture. Perhaps the reason for this is that country-style rooms are, above all, 'cosy' (in the sense of warm and relaxed comfort). This makes a great contrast to sparsely furnished ultra-modern homes, and other homes where there is a carefully planned blend of new and old.

Stripped pine furniture, simple dressers, rush-seated chairs, converted oil lamps and country-style fabrics are essential equipment for rooms of this type. Country furniture has changed little in design over the years. In Britain, for instance, rush-seated chairs similar to their 16th century forerunners are not hard to find.

Country furniture always looks attractive, and a well thought-out room of this type gives a warm and friendly atmosphere. This furniture is easy to find. Either it can be tracked down in junk shops, where it may well have come from a farmhouse, or it can be found in modern furnishing stores, where it will be spanking new, but made in the traditional designs or a modern variation. The good thing about new country furniture is that the larger pieces like dressers are scaled down in size so they are suitable for smaller homes, while the original pine dressers, tables and the like may well be on the large side for a small house.

Country furniture is an excellent buy for people on a tight budget. Much of it can be found hiding under layers of paint in second-hand shops. All that's needed is patience to strip away the old paint in order to bring up the original colour of the wood. The other essential is a good eye for spotting promising pieces of furniture that are not going to fall apart from woodworm or rot. Any good do-it-yourself carpenter will find it easy and inexpensive to make his own simple pine furniture. A small refectory table or a simple dresser are two ideas for a start. Add several dining chairs and a rocking chair, perhaps with some rustic fabric cushions. New polyurethane matt or gloss sealants make it a straightforward job if you want to give a clear, yet tough finish to either old or newly made pine furniture.

One more reason for the popularity of the country style is that as well as being totally different from modern room schemes, it is also far less expensive than some of the more extravagant styles of the past.

Country furniture is popular in most parts of the world, where styles are based on the simple rustic ideas of the past. In America, country furnishing ideas are often reminiscent of American Colonial days, while in France, the simple rustic styles of the French provinces are the inspiration.

With such a great freedom of choice, it is fun furnishing your home in a modern way. You can choose a sophisticated and totally modern style for your home, or there is the modern-plus-traditional style, or the country style. Each one can look 'right' and can be adapted to suit your specific needs.

The period touch— modern design : 2

Having established the interior design styles that are popular now, and the trends that have influenced their development, this chapter explains ways of giving a really modern look to your home.

The main point to remember when furnishing a room in the modern style is that there should be no clutter. Built-in cupboard and shelf units will take care of the bits and pieces, so that you only need the minimum in the way of furniture. Concentrate on colour and texture to help give the room extra style.

Rooms with a modern feeling can look good in both new and old houses. One of the most important items in a modern room is the lighting, and indirect lighting is now popular. Consider using track lights in a living room, recessed spot-

lights in a bedroom and downlighters in a dining room for dramatic effect. HOME DESIGNER 6 and 7 are full of good advice on this often awkward problem.

If you are looking for standard or table lamps, it is worth having one really stunning modern lamp as the final touch, so visit a top level department store first to get your eye in. You may be lucky enough to find a cheaper edition of a good modern light in a chain store, but if you can't find what you want there, save up for the more expensive one.

To help you get the idea of how to furnish a room in the three styles that are popular now, here are suggestions for a selection of room schemes to choose from. These can then be adapted to suit your particular preference— either totally modern, modern-plus-traditional, or country style.

In the living room

The first idea for a living room is a good one for a small home because it helps to give a great feeling of space. A good colour scheme would be emerald green and white with leather-covered chairs in brown or black. The floor-covering can be tailored to fit your pocket. Choose either a plain white fitted carpet, or sanded and sealed floorboards, or an inexpensive flooring like rush matting or sisal carpeting.

Make one wall a storage wall. The more the items stored are concealed, the greater the feeling of space. If there's a lot to hide, from books to a radio and drinks cupboard, make a line of tall plain doors to cover the entire wall. On a smaller scale, build a row of low shelves or low cupboards with plain doors, painted white. Don't decorate the cupboard tops with loads of ornaments or rows of books—just display a shapely potted plant or a jug of flowers and one or two pieces of modern pottery.

Use a tall floor-to-ceiling curtain to cover the whole of the window wall. Make the curtain in a nubbly loosely woven white fabric. Alternatively use plain white holland or Venetian blinds. Place a long low sofa against one wall, upholstered in a plain emerald green or white fabric or in

Below. A living room which incorporates many popular aspects of modern design. Note the bold colour scheme, streamlined storage unit and handsome lighting fittings.

Z.E.F.A.

Above. *A living room scheme decorated on a low budget, but with some effective modern touches. The red and white modular seating and table unit saves valuable space.*

Below. *A striking combination of old and new. The blue and white colour scheme is a perfect background for the elegant antique furniture in this modern living room.*

leather. Choose two or three easy chairs for the rest of the room. These should be in a light modern design to help create the modern atmosphere.

Paint the window wall and the wall opposite white. Paint the other two walls and the ceiling emerald green and choose recessed spotlights and one good standard lamp beside the settee. In one corner place a really tall potted plant. Place a long, low occasional table in front of the settee and group the other three chairs squarely round another low table. Keep pictures to the minimum; one or two large prints by contemporary artists would be ideal.

Another scheme for a modern living room is to give a plain brick finish to the fireplace wall. Choose an ultra-plain and narrow fireplace without a mantelpiece. Make a raised grate of plain white tiles or marble running along the whole wall, to provide a low shelf on either side of the fireplace. The shelf should be supported by a low natural brick wall one foot to eighteen inches high.

Make a feature of using the natural textures and add a pine-clad ceiling. The other walls can be painted white and the windows covered in either plain blinds or a floor-length semi-sheer curtain in a natural colour. For flooring choose a geometrically patterned fitted carpet in natural colours.

Place a long settee on each side of the fire. The backs of the settees can be against the walls if it is a small room. Upholster the settees in plain tweedy colours in a bright primary shade like scarlet. Put small square occasional tables at both ends of each settee and cover the tables with floor-length cloths of felt in a natural colour. On each table place a plain pottery lamp with a white drum shade or a low modern lamp of moulded plastic in white or red to match the settees.

In the middle of the floor between the two settees, place a large cube-shaped foam cushion, covered with mock fur or natural-coloured felt or velvet. Use one wall for storage, either in the form of a large and attractive antique cupboard, or in the form of modular units. Don't overcrowd wall space with pictures; use one large and striking modern one or a classical-looking picture without a frame.

An alternative scheme would be to keep the pine-clad ceiling, then to paint all the brick and plaster surfaces white. Have a shiny sanded floor, patterned with a colourful Persian rug. Show off brightly coloured books on one large open shelving unit. Cover easy chairs and the like in a bright textured fabric.

Built-in seating is popular for living rooms and looks good if it is made in natural materials. In front of an exposed brick wall in a living room, build a long low bench of matching bricks, topped with slate or pine. Place thick cushions along the bench for comfortable seating and add back cushions for a more luxurious effect. Use pine cladding for the other walls and the ceiling. To soften the effect, choose two large easy chairs of curly decorative basketwork or cane. Add a low pine table and a large plain blind for the window in a geometrical design. A plain tiled floor is a good choice. Use golds and woody colours for the cushions and a 'homespun' mat to help emphasize the brick and pine.

Another idea is to keep to a black and white theme, using black-painted occasional tables, a black or white storage unit, white upholstery and carpet, boldly patterned black and white curtains and metallic wallpaper, or one wall of aluminium foil and the rest painted white.

For a modern-plus-traditional scheme, use large cubes of foam for seating, then add a curvy Victorian buttoned chair. Keep all fabrics in the room modern. Use a big white shaggy rug to cover a plain stripped and sealed floor.

If you're building your own house, consider incorporating a seating pit into a living room plan. If not, and the room is a tall one, you could build up the floor level round the outside of the room to make a raised platform all the way round a central square or circle of deeply cushioned Fitted seats. Cover the cushioned seats in the same fabric as your curtains or one that matches your other furnishings.

A seating platform at one end of the room is another unusual idea. The floor of the platform is covered in carpet to match the rest of the room, and for additional seating use large floor cushions or slabs of foam covered in bright fabrics.

For a modern room with a country atmosphere, choose basketwork chairs and a matching settee. These have the advantage of being inexpensive, especially if you make your own cushions for the chairs. Choose a low pine occasional table. Pick a neat geometric wallpaper in brown and white, white curtains, cushions in plain primary colours and a Japanese globular paper lamp hung low from the ceiling in one corner of the room.

It is important to keep the design of a room fluid, so that it can be adapted easily to suit the needs of the moment. Some of the newest seating gives exciting possibilities for this. There are easy chairs without arms and matching corner chairs that have one arm and a straight back. These can be juxtaposed to make perhaps one long sofa down one side of the room, an L-shaped seating arrangement, and so on—there are plenty of variations.

One good thing about these chairs is that you can buy them one at a time, as and when you can afford it. Exciting possibilities for using colour emerge. Try a two-colour scheme for an L-shaped arrangement of chairs, with a white chair in the corner, flanked by deep blue ones. Hang a cluster of lights low over a corner table, paint the walls and floor white, add bright cotton curtains in a bold geometric pattern and a Spanish rug on the floor.

For a budget room, choose sack chairs, shiny blow-up chairs or large and brightly patterned floor cushions with a low pine or perspex table, plain white walls, rattan blind and sanded and sealed floor.

In the dining room

For an inexpensive dining room scheme, choose a plain wooden table, painted white or bright red. Add folding director's chairs with natural-coloured canvas seats and red woodwork. Use a red- or white-painted chest of drawers as a dresser and above it hang a large carved mirror bought from a junk shop, with its frame painted white. Cover one wall with scarlet hessian and paint the other walls white.

Above. An Italian look has been given to this modern dining room, with its white acrylic furniture and honey-coloured floor tiles. Note the clever use of black to highlight the shape of the room.
Below. A modern dining room with a country look—and a country outlook. The extensive use of natural wood is most effective.

Z.E.F.A.

MICHAEL BOYS

Choose shiny white vinyl tiles for the floor. A tall pot plant completes the picture.

Select a modern table and cane chairs as an alternative scheme. On one wall use a bold geometric paper. Pick out one of the colours from the paper—like a deep chestnut brown—and use this colour for the ceiling. Paint the rest of the walls white. Use a moulded plastic shade for a light hanging low over the table, or a well-designed rise and fall light. Choose either a deep brown fitted carpet, or plain floorboards, stripped and sealed, depending on your budget. Contrast the scheme with a nineteenth century painting, unframed, to dominate one wall.

For a ritzy scheme, select a shiny metallic wallpaper to use on both the walls and the ceiling. Add long plain white curtains with plain borders. As the centrepiece choose shiny metal-framed chairs and table in a sculptured modern design, the table with a glass top. A plain nubbly carpet in a russet colour will add warmth. As a sideboard, choose a second tall glass-topped table, so that you keep to the modern theme.

Alternatively make a room with a panelled effect by hanging long floor-to-ceiling blinds of rattan. Make hardboard frames painted lime green for the blinds. Add a modern table in chrome or moulded plastic with either moulded pedestal dining chairs or folding ones with chrome frames and clear perspex seats. Paint the floor to match the frames for the blinds or choose a carpet to match the colour.

Country-style dining rooms are fun to make and there are plenty of variations on the theme of pine dresser, table and chairs with rush seats. Louvred shutters at the windows look good in a room like this. Alternatively choose a matching wallpaper and curtain fabric, which can also be used on a fringed table cloth. Ceramic-tiled floor, close carpets or stripped and sealed boards are three floorings that would be ideal, so take your choice and buy the one that suits your pocket the best. Make your own country-style table with a pine frame and legs and a ceramic-tiled top. Use the same tiles effectively in alcoves or in one corner with plain pine or glass open shelves to display ornaments.

Choose bentwood chairs or pine benches and a pine refectory table. Use horizontal pine cladding on one wall. Paint other walls white and use one to display a collection of pictures.

Make your own modern painting for a modern-plus-traditional room. Cut a 4ft square piece of plywood or hardboard into an 'amoeba' shape, or into the shape of an apple, then paint it with bold three-inch wide diagonal stripes in a striking colour combination like daffodil yellow and scarlet.

In the bedroom

Make the accent on built-in furniture for a modern bedroom. Use one wall for storage and select or make your own built-in clothes storage unit that incorporates a vanitory unit, dressing table and even a small work corner. To save space in a small bedroom-cum-workroom, build the bed up high so that the work table can be slid away underneath it when not in use.

For a cool scheme in neutral colours, have a storage wall with plain or louvred doors, all painted white. Add a neutral coloured carpet, creamy coloured walls and white paintwork and plain white blinds with a neutral-coloured strip of border. Choose a low divan bed and cover it with a luxurious bedspread made from fake fur. Choose a cane table and chair for a dressing table and fix a white perspex-framed mirror above it. On either side of the bed place two low occasional tables of canework with glass tops. Use either small modern moulded plastic table lamps beside the bed, or low hanging lamps over each table. Keep walls uncluttered apart from perhaps a hanging canvas hold-all or a closely grouped collection of pictures.

Try a blue and white scheme. Use boldly striped blue and white wallpaper on all the walls as well as the cupboard doors which will then merge into the wall. At the window use a plain white blind or white curtains. Choose a plain deep blue carpet. Cover the low divan bed with a plain white tailored bedspread. Hang a 'headboard' of the matching fabric on a deep blue-painted wooden pole behind the bed. Add lots of scatter cushions with bold striped or triangular patterned covers. On either side of the bed place blue-painted low chests of drawers. A modern chair on chrome legs will complete the picture, in front of a plain table with a glass top to use for make-up and the like.

For the 'unfurnished' look, make a low platform for the bed, carpeted to match the rest of the room. On the platform, place a large foam mattress covered either in a tweedy fabric or with a fake fur bedspread. Add more scatter cushions, vertical blinds at the window and a modern-looking light on a low cube-shaped table. Unify all storage such as the dressing table behind a row of plain doors or blinds. As with so many modern rooms, the final touch is a tall, leafy potted plant.

For a country-style bedroom, choose matching wallpaper, curtains and bedspread, a brass bed, one pine-clad wall, and a deep-pile fitted carpet. Choose modern fitted cupboards and storage units and one or two modern bedside tables. An old pine wash stand for a dressing table and old oil lamps are the finishing touches.

All these ideas help to underline the great freedom of choice for furnishing a home. Many families in small homes gain space by knocking out walls and making a large multi-purpose room for living, eating and working. Modular unit furniture is ideally suited for rooms of this type and you could combine some of the ideas in this feature for your own multi-purpose room.

Below. *An all-brown colour scheme gives a warm look to this modern bedroom. The Italian influence is typified by the bed platform and shelf unit, and fur bedspread.*

GRAZIA NERI

An Introduction to Antiques and Price Guide

Alphabetical Guide to Antiques

VICTORIAN GOTHIC BENCH There was a persistent search for novelty in the nineteenth century. One aspect of this was the passion for reviving past styles. In search of an identity, the newly prosperous favoured in turn the Jacobean, Elizabethan and French François I styles and finally the Gothic, which had already attained a certain popularity in the previous century.

There was difficulty in resuscitating the Gothic in that practically no original, Medieval Gothic furniture had survived, so a style had to be invented using the vocabulary of Gothic architecture which included pinnacles and crockets (the bird or leaf ornaments on the sides of pinnacles) and pointed arches. These decorative features are illustrated in the bench here.

'The Gothick', as it is sometimes called, was particularly suitable for solemn, masculine pieces of furniture for dining rooms, libraries or halls. The bench illustrated here was made in about 1850 and was obviously designed for an entrance hall. A seventeenth century feature, the twisted members are known as 'barley-sugar turned'. The bench is 6ft 10in. high and 4ft 3½in. wide and is made of oak with an elm seat on which there is an inscription.

Associated with the revival of Gothic motifs was a renewed interest in narrative detail like that found in sculpture on the façade and interior of some Gothic ecclesiastical buildings. This detail can be seen in contemporary paintings of pre-Raphaelites and also in woodcarvings on furniture. Some of the best known examples are sideboards with doors characterized by elaborate and often high-quality woodcarving.

In this bench, the sleeping figures are confined to the top of the back, where there is no wear from or discomfort to the user. It is evident that these figures were conceived as corresponding to the sculpture on a Gothic cathedral, interposed in the architectural framework.

Victorian button-backed chair £125

Glen Dewart, London.

Cooper-Bridgeman Library

VICTORIAN BUTTON-BACKED CHAIR The button-backed chair was the 'easy chair' of the Victorian period. Firmly upholstered and elegant, it was found in most comfortable middle-class homes.

The technique of buttoning had been introduced in the second half of the eighteenth century as a device to give fresh decorative character to upholstered furniture and, also, to increase comfort when leather was used as a covering.

Although primarily a decorative device, the method of buttoning was favoured, particularly by the practical Victorians, because of its hard-wearing and resilient surface. The back and feet of the chair or sofa were well padded and then covered with light canvas. The material was stretched into place more loosely than it was for ordinary upholstered work before it was attached to the outer frame.

Strong thread was then stitched through the padding and outer case to the back. The stitches were pulled in tightly to draw the padding and covering into a form of quilting and then hidden by a button, usually of the same material as the cover. The chair or sofa back was finally covered to conceal the stitching that had been taken through from the front. The buttons were disposed in a regular pattern, generally in the form of elongated diamonds and half-diamonds, though squares were used occasionally.

The Victorian button-backed chair illustrated here has a carved walnut frame and stands on cabriole legs with castors. It has been re-upholstered in velvet, but the original upholstery was probably a crushed velvet, giving a fairly similar appearance. It is likely that the chair was designed for a gentleman and may well have originally been matched by a smaller companion for a lady.

VICTORIAN GROUP

The sofa table shown in this group is of a type that was particularly popular in the Regency period, though they were also made in the early Victorian period. A development of the Pembroke table, and made popular by Sheraton, they were generally between five and six feet long, and from twenty-two to twenty-four inches wide. An ideal size for placing alongside a sofa, they were used for writing, drawing and reading. The example shown here is made of mahogany and banded with rosewood. It has two drawers, and the top is supported by turned columns and inward curved legs with traditional lion paw feet.

The chairs in the group are typical mid-Victorian button-backed chairs which have recently been re-upholstered in Dralon velvet. Button-backed chairs tend to need this treatment as the buttons place a strain on the fabric. The chairs shown are part of a set of four designed for use in the dining room.

The copper tea urn was ideal for large Victorian families. It provides an attractive cache-pot or can be used on its own as an ornament.

VICTORIAN SIDE-CABINET AND CLOCK This satinwood side-cabinet is a good example of the delicately painted and parcel-gilt furniture that became popular in the mid-Victorian period. Its graceful lines were made in imitation of the neo-classical furniture of the late eighteenth century. D-shaped in section view, it has a velvet-covered wooden top with projecting applied pilasters, a centre cupboard, and curved open shelves at the sides. It dates from about 1860 and is stamped Lamb and numbered 12702.

The fragility is not confined to the decoration. All the raised work is executed in gesso—a composition of parchment, size and whiting that chips as easily as a plaster cast. The vine border at the base of the cabinet is painted gesso. The rest of the painted decoration consists of oval medallions with dancing nymphs and a frieze with a central panel depicting Cupid.

The clock on top of the cabinet has an earthenware case made by Wedgwood, the factory with one of the longest records of constant production in England. The factory was founded by Josiah Wedgwood in 1759 and it is still operating today. Although better known for its tableware, Wedgwood also produced earthenware busts and other assorted objects during the nineteenth century. This clock has an arched top and moulded pillars. It is decorated with blue-painted landscapes on the front and sides in the manner of Delft ware. On the wall is an oil painting of a river scene by Clarkson Stanfield, a noted Victorian painter.

GILLOW DESK. Gillow's are one of the oldest and most reputable firms connected with English furniture production. They were founded in 1695 in Lancaster. In 1761 the business moved to Oxford Street in London where they remained until 1906.

At first Gillow's were architects—they were responsible for the design of the eighteenth century Custom House at Lancaster—as well as cabinet makers. Two of their best known furniture designers were Sheraton and Hepplewhite.

The firm carried out designs of their own invention; the original billiard table was conceived and made by Gillow's. About 1800 they patented the telescopic dining table. They also made a special type of writing table for Captain Davenport, who gave his name to this piece of furniture.

The firm's records go back as far as 1731. After 1820 nearly every piece of furniture they made was numbered and stamped with their name, as shown here. It is comparatively easy, therefore, to identify their Victorian models.

The desk pictured here is made of mahogany with some carved decoration. It has an original, stamped leather top which can be either flat for writing or, as illustrated, adjusted for reading. The gallery and handles are made of brass.

VICTORIAN REVOLVING BOOKCASE The storage of books can be a problem. It is difficult to arrange them so that all the spines are visible and they are all readily accessible. The traditional and simplest means is shelving applied to the wall. Special library steps—sometimes disguised as chairs— were designed and made in the eighteenth century to enable the top shelves to be reached.

It was in about 1800 that the small and extremely practical revolving bookcase was invented. It was designed as a free-standing object for the library. The earliest and best examples are composed of circular shelves which revolve around a central column. The difficulty was, of course, that the books had to be inserted at an angle, but this was overcome by the addition of wedge-shaped blocks, inserted at intervals.

The bookcase illustrated here, made about 1870, is an adaptation of the Regency type. It is less attractive but in many ways more practical since, apart from the centre shaft, there is no space that is impossible to use. It is made of mahogany and has an inlay of ivory and exotic woods.

It is usually easy to distinguish Victorian copies of Regency or earlier furniture from the colour and wear on the wood. In addition, the manufacture and craftsmanship differ. No Georgian or Regency piece would display the studs that are so evident here. One of the characteristics of modern design lies in the fact that no attempt is made to camouflage the basic structure.

Print-stand £325.

Jeffrey R. Dell, London.   Cooper-Bridgeman Library.

VICTORIAN PRINT-STAND AND MUSIC STAND An antique object is classified as rare for a number of different reasons. Often a piece that was originally made in quantity becomes unusual, or even unique, because the other examples have simply worn out or been broken; obviously this is most frequently the case with items made in fragile materials such as porcelain and glass. Sometimes a piece was rare initially, and commissioned from the maker for a specific place or purpose, although perhaps adapted from a standard design. Many of the finest pieces of furniture are certainly rare for this reason as well as for reasons of quality.

This print-stand belongs to the latter category because, although it is not grand or expensive, as far as is known there was never a great demand for such a specialised piece of furniture, appealing only to serious collectors of prints. Examples that do exist, with rare exceptions, have no base compartment for storing prints. This is a feature of the one illustrated, and probably derives from a canterbury. The sides of the upper section are adjustable on the principle of the sides of a hay wain. Hinged at the base, each side can be raised or lowered according to the size of the collection.

The wood is walnut, and stained to a comparatively deep colour. The spiral turned columns are known as barley twist, and the decorated side panels of the base were achieved with a fret saw.

CYLINDER BUREAU A bureau is a distinctive type of writing desk, designed so that the writing surface, the racks of pigeon holes and drawers and all the paraphernalia of writing can be disguised. Early examples of this furniture had a simple hinged flap for this purpose. Later, sliders, narrow pieces of wood that pull out from the corners of the bureau, were incorporated to support the flap. A model of this design is known as a drop- or fall-front bureau and is usually found combined with a chest of drawers as the base. A variation of this is a drawer that is pulled out and the front lowered to provide a working surface. A late eighteenth-century development was the roll, tambour or cylinder top, as shown here.

This example is made of mahogany and has a kneehole base with a single drawer flanked by pedestals with three graduated doors and a cupboard in the kneehole. Above the quarter cylinder front is a concave frieze. The interior is fitted with horn-handled drawers and pigeon holes. The baize lined sliding writing surface is bordered by mahogany cross banding. The bureau is just over 4ft wide and has bracket feet and brass loop handles and lock plates.

The bureau shown here is a well made Victorian version of a neat Georgian piece of the Sheraton period, a period that produced many new types and styles of furniture. Victorian designers adapted these styles to make the furniture more functional and to facilitate its production for the mass market.

Desk £95, Staffordshire dogs £21

Peter Jones, London S.W.1 Cooper-Bridgeman Library

VICTORIAN KNEE-HOLE DESK The term 'knee-hole' refers to the space between the drawer supports of a writing-table. Although this type desk was invented by the Victorians, it has its origins in the late seventeenth century when the first tables designed specifically for writing were made in England.

The desk is constructed in three sections: the top section, having three drawers, and the two side sections, each having three-drawer pedestals. This construction and the castors on which the desk is mounted, make it easy to dismantle or move. It is made of oak with mahogany drawer linings and has its original leather top. Oak is generally stained to a dark colour, a practice begun in Tudor times and continued to this day. Here, however, the wood has been polished, not stained, and retains its natural colour. It is one of the hardest and heaviest woods used in cabinet-making and the colour is affected by the soil in which the tree grew.

Dating from about 1850, this piece is absolutely without ornament. There are no mouldings and even the turned wooden drawer knobs are of the simplest type. It exemplifies the fact that good proportions can suffice to give a pleasing appearance.

The pair of spaniels are probably Staffordshire, although a similar mould was used at Sunderland. The gilt decoration dates them to the latter part of the nineteenth century as untarnishable gilding was a fairly late development. The dogs were popular models and made in considerable numbers. Not more than two casts, or possibly three in the summer, could be made in a day because of the time that had to be allowed for drying. Up to about two hundred casts could be made from each mould before the detail was lost.

NEEDLEWORK PICTURES

Decorative needlework was on the decline at the beginning of the eighteenth century but fresh incentive was given in the middle of the century, by the emergence of a talented and active group of engravers. Needlewomen were reminded of the charm of such painters as Morland, Copley and Westall and they in their turn copied the painters, producing beautifully worked pictures in spun-silk, silk twist or chenille.

Some of the most highly prized of these pictures were those that combined needlework with painting. By this method, the designed scene was first sketched in water-colour on to a plain piece of satin or silk and the face and hands of the figures left untouched; the rest of the picture was heavily worked with the needle to create the impression of a relief. Alternatively, the hands and faces were sometimes cut from an engraving and stuck on to the satin, or else the process was reversed and the uncovered areas were stitched and the rest merely pasted down.

The age, and hence the value of a picture can often be gauged as much from the quality of its mount and frame as from the picture itself. Its price is often determined by subject matter as well as by quality. A picture after Morland, for example, tends to fetch much more than a picture after an undistinguished contemporary.

Private collection   Cooper-Bridgeman Library

Needlework pictures can cost from £12 upwards.

John Luddington and Eric Hardy-Smith, Chelsea Antique Market, London SW3   Cooper-Bridgeman Library

VICTORIAN FIRE SCREENS

Victorian ladies liked to think of themselves as having delicate complexions, which needed to be protected from the heat of a fire. It was for this purpose that the fire screen was invented; screens were also used in summer to hide the empty grate. Like all Victorian furniture, these fire screens were decorative as well as functional. More substantial, but less ornamental metal screens were also used directly in front of the grate to stop flying sparks from setting fire to the carpet.

Victorian fire screens are found in many shapes and sizes. The tall one shown here is of the type known as a pole screen. Its height is adjustable, and it was intended for use as a face protector at some distance from the fire. The shorter, larger screen is a cheval screen, so called because, like a cheval mirror, it has a 'horse-like' four-legged frame.

Other types of fire screen include hand-held ones like fans; these were often made of papier-mâché. There were also banner screens that were fixed to the mantelpiece, and had adjustable extending arms.

The screens in the picture both date from the middle of the nineteenth century. They have mahogany frames containing panels of canvas work decoration; the pole screen is done in gros point (large cross stitch) and the cheval screen in tent stitch. Tapestry work and embroidery were popular Victorian pastimes, and fire screens were often made to match cushions and upholstery. Berlin wool-work, another kind of canvas work in coloured worsteds or silk which included glass beads, was also very fashionable at the time, and the first printed patterns were produced for this by a firm in Germany.

David Pettifer Ltd, London, S.W.3. The Cooper-Bridgeman Library

Mid-nineteenth-century tripod table: £110. Tea-caddy: £18. Bread-basket: £35.

PAPIER MACHE

Although small papier-mâché articles such as tobacco or snuff-containers were made in England in the eighteenth century, papier mâché is more generally associated with the Victorian period. The growth in the industry was largely due to Henry Clay's invention of a new hard, heat-resistant paperware that he patented in 1772 and which was much tougher and more durable than anything produced previously. When Clay's Birmingham factory was taken over by Jennens and Bettridge in 1816, the new firm began the large-scale manufacture of household furnishings, making numerous articles.

The heyday of papier mâché was the period between 1830 and 1860. As the centre of the trade shifted from Birmingham to London, so the quality of the work declined. In 1864 Jennens and Bettridge closed down and, although cheap papier mâché continued to be made, it became brittle and coarse.

It is unusual to find an identifying mark on any of the smaller pieces of papier mâché. The value of each item depends on its shape, condition and quality of decoration and these factors also help to determine the date of a piece. The later and cheaper examples can be recognized by their lightness and the surface gloss which is markedly different from the deep shine of later work.

A small application of liquid furniture cream provides the best method of cleaning papier mâché; soap and detergent are both inadvisable.

PAPIER-MACHE DRESSING TABLE Papier-mâché was a popular material in the nineteenth century, and was used for all kinds of articles from small ornaments right up to sofas and piano casings. Although it is made out of paper, papier-mâché is much tougher than it looks. Its slight flexibility keeps it from chipping, and the stronger varieties are completely resistant to heat and damp. But thin, easily-snapped parts such as legs must be made of wood or metal.

Commercially-made Victorian papier-mâché was manufactured by soaking sheets of special paper in a mixture of paste and glue and pressing them together in a mould. This made a thin board, which was allowed to dry and then built up to the required thickness by adding other layers in the same way. It was then hardened by dipping it in oil, after which it could be sawn, and even planed, like ordinary wood. The surface was finished with coloured varnish—usually black but occasionally red or white—inlaid with slivers of mother of pearl.

This elaborately-decorated dressing table forms part of a suite of papier-mâché bedroom furniture. The inlay and gilding work are unusually complex, but the basic shape is a series of fairly simple curves, with far less moulding than a wooden piece of the same date. This boldness in design is a characteristic of the best papier-mâché work of the period, which shows quite clearly that it has been made in a mould and not by a cabinet-maker.

BOOKCASE Some furniture, such as chairs and most tables, is designed to be placed in the middle of a room and viewed from all angles. Some, on the other hand, is designed to be set against a wall. In this case the back is not polished, and is only roughly finished. This bookcase falls into the second category.

You can discover quite a lot about the age and quality of this type of furniture by looking at the back. For example, this bookcase is in the Regency style, and if it were genuine, it would have been made in the first two decades of the 19th century. But this particular example is a good-quality Victorian reproduction; the Victorians often copied earlier styles of furniture.

The time lapse between original and copy is not very long in this case, so the differences are not pronounced. Genuine Regency furniture is very accurately and solidly made, and a later copy would probably be flimsier and less well-fitting; this would show clearly at the back. The thickness of the veneer can also be seen from this side. Victorian veneer is mostly under $\frac{1}{16}$ in. thick; Regency veneer much thicker.

Many Victorian copies had bad proportions, but this is quite a good example. It has ormolu (gilded base metal) mounts and a quilted silk lining.

The carved and painted figure of St Luke is Italian and dates from about 1870. The books have leather bindings.

Bookcase £58; sculpture £30

Crewe Read and Partners, New King's Road, London. Cooper-Bridgeman Library

Axe drop 1660-1710

Pear drop 1660-1710

Acorn drop 1660-1710

Engraved plate 1700

Solid plate 1700

Pierced plate 1710

Anno Domini Antiques

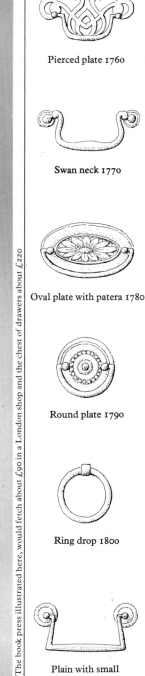

Pierced plate 1760

Swan neck 1770

Oval plate with patera 1780

Round plate 1790

Ring drop 1800

Plain with small black plates 1800

c. 1790. The book press illustrated here, would fetch about £90 in a London shop and the chest of drawers about £220

CHEST OF DRAWERS AND BOOK PRESS. This finely proportioned small Sheraton chest of drawers in rich faded mahogany has high bracket feet and a brushing slide, a sliding tray originally used for gentlemen's hairbrushes. As a piece of furniture it served as the gentlemen's equivalent in his dressing room to a lady's dressing table in her bedroom. This particular piece still has its original handles; a likely indication that they had been replaced by reproduction handles or those in a later style would have been the fabrication of another hole or a different, newer type of nut at the back.

The chest of drawers is surmounted by a mahogany book press with light mahogany banding. This would have been used to hold leather bound books in the days before cloth bindings were used and the handling of a book was a delicate affair.

THE ARTS AND CRAFTS MOVEMENT was a nineteenth century revival of the craftsmanship of the eighteenth century, to encourage co-operation between the crafts. William Morris was one of its main instigators. The chairs, wall-brackets and pots shown here were all made by craftsmen sympathetic to the ideals of the Movement. To recognize furniture of the period, look for ebonized wood, spindle-turning and hand-painted and gilt panels. Different in appearance from most late Victorian pieces, Arts and Crafts furniture is often not recognized by dealers for what it is.

Most recognizable and popular of the Arts and Crafts pieces are the pots. On the left is a stoneware vase made by Robert Wallace Martin. He and his brothers specialized in stoneware—known as Martinware—grotesque in decoration and form, often with a crude encrusted surface. The earthenware vase on the right was designed by Dr. Christopher Dresser for the Linthorpe Pottery, Middlesbrough. His glass, metal-work and pottery is beginning to fetch high prices.

The functional, unsophisticated, 'no-nonsense' character of Arts and Crafts pieces is most appealing to the present taste for simplicity, and a quick eye could discover many bargains.

COUNTRY FURNITURE This group of eighteenth century country furniture is as well suited to the functional, uncluttered interior of a country cottage as it ever was, and usually provides a better investment than any modern equivalent.

The small side table, which has an elm top on an oak base, is embellished with a scalloped apron and the straight legs are connected by an H-stretcher. As is often the case, the handles have been changed at a later date by a fashion-conscious owner. This can be detected by looking at the interior of the drawer for indications of old holes to which the original plate was fixed. Another point to bear in mind is that elmwood, like fruitwood, is particularly prone to woodworm, and any piece which has been badly affected is obviously not a good buy. Examples in oak are generally cheaper than those in other woods, and the price of a simple country table is often proportionate to the size as well as the quality of its workmanship, smaller pieces costing correspondingly more on account of greater demand.

The chairs are generally described as Lancashire spindle-back chairs, although they are known to have been made elsewhere in the North. A clue that these particular examples were actually made in Lancashire is provided by the spindles being bunched towards the middle of the back, leaving gaps at each end of the row. The two club feet resting on turned balls are a characteristic feature of this type of chair. Rush chairs constitute a safe buy, since fakes are virtually unknown. They are almost always cheaper when bought in sets rather than in pairs.

The blue and white bowl is made of Liverpool delft, a generally unsophisticated type of pottery which blends well with an interior furnished in the country style.

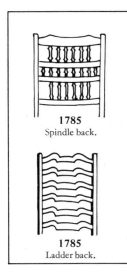

1785
Spindle back.

1785
Ladder back.

Buffet £175; pair of vases £20

Phelps Ltd, 129-135 St. Margaret's Road, Twickenham   Cooper-Bridgeman Library

VICTORIAN BUFFET This massive oak sideboard is elaborately decorated with carving, most of which depicts sporting trophies. For this reason, it seems likely that it was made for the dining room of a country house.

A buffet is defined as a piece of furniture with cupboards in the base and shelves in the upper section. But the basic form of this one is almost completely hidden by the enormous amount of carved decoration. A Victorian critic of this kind of furniture complained: 'The designer has constructed ornament and forgotten use altogether and the result is shown in a heap of massive, rich and useless furniture, sideboards that will display nothing but the skill of the carver, and cabinets that are too often a museum of natural curiosities in themselves.'

Woodcarving was a popular Victorian hobby. Queen Victoria approved of it, and at her Jubilee presented testimonials in caskets carved by amateurs. Many elaborately carved objects were displayed at the Great Exhibition of 1851, one of which, a cradle, was sent by the Queen herself.

This buffet is not the work of an amateur, however, but a thoroughly well-executed piece of professional work. The style of the oval medallions on the doors is inspired by Grinling Gibbons, the great seventeenth-century wood carver who created, among other things, the carvings in St. Paul's cathedral.

Ornate Victorian furniture of this type is currently enjoying a revival in popularity. In an otherwise bare and plain modern setting, the sheer richness and textural interest of this buffet would turn it into an impressive centre-piece.

The blue and white vases are Oriental.

VICTORIAN CREDENZA A mirror attached to a cupboard. At first sight this appears to be a dressing-table, but three considerations place it as an example of Victorian dining-room furniture: the height of the mirror—nearly four feet from floor level—and the fact that it is not adjustable, and the central cupboard in the base, all of which would make it impossible to use from a seated position.

In the 1840's, the projecting base of the medieval or Elizabethan credenza, a side table on which food and drink were placed before being served at table, was revived; and to it was often added a mirror in the upper section. It retained its function as a temporary resting-place for plates and is therefore quite distinct from another popular type of Victorian sideboard which was designed to display china and decorative wares on shelves and ledges in the manner of a Welsh dresser.

This particular credenza would have been an expensive piece at the time of its manu-facture. Made of mahogany and walnut veneer, the fretwork which appears to support the mirror-glass—it in fact rests on the top of the base with the fretwork super-imposed—is well executed and the hand carving of the mirror supports and medallion frame are extremely fine in quality. This was a time of great interest in wood carving, particularly in naturalistic subjects and motifs, exemplified by a sideboard in the Victoria and Albert Museum, London, depicting the story of Robinson Crusoe. It became difficult, at that point, to distinguish between furniture and sculpture.

The brass candlesticks are also Victorian, of a standard design and mass produced.

VICTORIAN STOOLS The great variety in the appearance of nineteenth-century furniture is due partly to the genuine inventiveness of the designers of the time and partly to the fact that almost the entire range of forms and styles of furniture from the past were revived and adapted. Stools, one of the very earliest forms of furniture, were made in an apparently unending number of differing styles, particularly piano, or music, stools.

The two illustrated here (centre and right), dating from the mid-century, are made of ebonized wood, wood stained black in imitation of ebony. The essential constructional feature of piano stools is the device for raising or lowering the height of the seat. The four-legged stool with turned members has a knob at either side connected to a metal wheel and cog mechanism beneath the seat; the one with the machine-carved tripod base, a type that was also made in brass, works on the screw principle, and it is the ancestor of the swivelling office chair.

The stool on the left with scroll feet probably formed part of a set of seat furniture. It was made in about 1870. The cabriole legs derive from early eighteenth-century furniture. The attenuated form of this birch piece is close to Art Nouveau.

The upholstery, of leather, needlework, velvet or some other fabric, is often to be found damaged, but it is usually not difficult to repair the worn patches or re-cover the seat in similar material.

VICTORIAN CHAISE LONGUE One of the most comfortable postures for reading is reclining, with head and elbows supported. It was partly for this purpose that the Victorian chaise longue was created. In Loudon's *Encyclopaedia* of 1846 it was described as wanting in elegance, but, claim the editors, 'we can assert, from experience, that it is exceedingly comfortable to sit on'.

Chaise longue translated into English means couch or daybed. In Sheraton's words: 'These have their name from the French, which imports a long chair'. They were, in fact, used more for relaxing than reading—'Their use is to rest or loll upon after dinner'. The standard drawing room chair was considerably less comfortable than those of today and this probably explains why the chaise longue is not in common use now.

The chaise longue illustrated here forms part of a suite of walnut furniture dating from about 1860. As is often the case, the carving and cabriole legs are evidence of French influence. The chaise longue owed its mid-century popularity to a revival in France by the Empress Eugénie, wife of Napoleon III and a leader of European fashion.

The width of the upholstered seat accommodated the fullness of feminine dress at that time. Whether a seat for reading or for ladies to recline upon, the chaise longue was a comfortable and popular adjunct to the Victorian home.

BRACKET CLOCK

Originally this clock was made with brackets fixed to the wall: it usually had a drawer for the winding key. Few of these ensembles survive and gradually more clocks of a similar type were made without the brackets. Today the term 'bracket clock' generally is used to describe any clock that stands on a mantel or table.

The maker of this example, J. Rose, departed from the design of a traditional Georgian bracket clock only in the gothicizing of the mahogany case. The circular dial, brass handles, ball feet and matching finial vary little from an earlier timepiece. It is remarkable that so few details—the elongated arches, quatrefoil motif and the capitals of the columns—could convert a standard object to the prevailing taste in the early nineteenth century for the Gothic. It can be seen from this that a piece of furniture needs only the most superficial alterations to give it an exotic or currently popular flavour. At the Great Exhibition of 1851, the precedent for the Festival of Britain of 1951, clocks were given an Egyptian, Jacobean, Elizabethan and even French Louis Quinze appearance by similar simple ornamental divergences.

This clock was made to strike at the hour and it has a deadbeat escapement. The escapement is the mechanism that releases and locks the wheel which controls the weight or pendulum at regular intervals.

The deadbeat escapement was invented at the beginning of the eighteenth century by English maker, George Graham, and because it is one of the most reliable, it is still employed in some domestic clocks today.

AMERICAN SQUARE CLOCK

This wall clock in an ogee-sectioned case with a finely-figured walnut veneer is from the American firm of Jerome and Company, one of the most successful producers in the nineteenth century of cheap wall clocks. They were mass produced in America and exported in the 1830s in enormous numbers to meet the new demand from factories and working-class homes following the Industrial Revolution. They eventually posed such a threat to English makers that the Customs prohibited their import.

The early American square clocks are generally eight-day clocks and have wooden movements. A cheaper, thirty-hour clock with a factory-made, rolled-brass movement, like the example illustrated here, was designed and produced by Jerome.

These clocks are generally reliable, and not expensive even if bought in good working condition; this is particularly important since they can cost more than their value to repair. The maker's name and directions for setting up the clock are usually shown inside, and these should be complete. The glass painting below the clock dial should be undamaged and note should be taken of the subject; ballooning scenes, for example, invariably add to the value of the clock.

The line drawings shown here illustrate contemporary English wall clocks which are fairly easy to come by, but possibly not as decorative as their American equivalents.

The American clock in prime working condition would cost about £32.

Glass-fronted cabinet £125

CORNER CABINET Corner cupboards are specifically designed for the corners of a room and fitted with solid doors. In the type of cupboard illustrated here, the upper portion has been glazed for the purpose of displaying china, and is generally described as a cabinet.

Original records of corner cupboards appeared in the first half of the seventeenth century. In Charles I's inventory, reference is made to 'one little three cornered cupboard'. Not until the reign of William and Mary were corner cupboards adopted for general use. They were initially used for storing china, particularly the novel and highly prized tea services which are being made today. Soon, however, the china was put on display and, from about 1750, glazed china cabinets also became plentiful. Panelling was very much in vogue in the eighteenth century and corner and alcove cupboards often formed part of the deal panelling of a room. 'Every corner', wrote the contemporary diarist Celia Fiennes, 'is improved for cupboards and necessaries, and the doors to them made suitable to the wainscot.' It is interesting that, although the Victorians introduced the fashion for large pieces of movable furniture, we have since re-adopted the Georgian predilection for fitted furniture, although for different reasons.

This particular mahogany cabinet was made in the nineteenth century when production was largely confined to the provinces and the pieces made by country craftsmen tended to be coarsely carved and inlaid. It is made in two sections, the lower section containing a shelved cupboard, and stands on neat ball feet. Its appearance has been altered recently by the addition of two brass handles to the glass doors and a brass escutcheon to the lower section, but these have not significantly affected its value.

The plates displayed in the cupboard are made by Mason's Patent Ironstone China Ltd. They are reproductions of a traditional design called 'Romantic', produced by the original firm, Masons of Lane Delph, founded in 1813, and famous for their stone china.

VICTORIAN BOOKCASE

This fine piece is made of tulipwood and satinwood. Both woods are imported and first used in English cabinet-making in the eighteenth century. Tulipwood is the harder and heavier of the two and used here for the cross-banding and for the semi-circular glazing bars. The paler, softer, figured satinwood is used for the panelling. The upper section has a mirrored scroll cresting above an over-hanging frieze which has drop finials made of ivory. The projecting lower section has two drawers above a cup-board.

The height from the top of the pediment to the ground is just over 7ft 6in. which, though tall, makes it by no means an exceptionally large bookcase of this type. Robert Adam designed one for a London house that is 11ft in height, and there are some that are even taller. The proportion of glazing to panelling is standard and derives from an eighteenth century model. In the eighteenth century this large and imposing model often formed an integral part of the interior decoration of a room. The height of the sill of the projecting section corresponds to the height of the chair rail, and the whole is treated architecturally with columns and pediments.

A variant of this type of case, and one much favoured by the Victorians, is the bureau-bookcase, in which the drawer is equipped as a writing desk with a drop front. This functional detail serves to make it a more expensive piece of furniture today.

Bookcase £470

SHAVING STAND AND POT-LID

The shaving stand became popular in England in the early years of the nineteenth century and is one of the few pieces of furniture designed and made entirely for masculine use.

Several variants of this small table fitted with a swivel mirror exist, reflecting the many fashions in furniture and design adopted and then rejected by the Victorians. This example, made of mahogany, dates from the mid-nineteenth century. Although the pedestal and foot are composed of a mixture of different decorative and constructional idioms, the piece is comparatively restrained in style.

The pot-lid, from a container of Naples shaving paste, might well have been used by a Victorian gentleman in conjunction with the shaving stand. The period during which pot-lids were produced was approximately 1847 to 1880, although up to a few years ago copies were still being reproduced from the original copper plates. The differences are fairly obvious, the main points to look for in the reproductions being a rather heavier texture than is usually found in genuine lids, paler colours, artificially large crazing and thick rims.

Shaving stand would cost about £54 and pot-lids from £8 to £850 largely depending on rarity.

CHEVAL MIRROR. Cheval mirrors are called after the French word for horse, and are also sometimes known as 'horse' dressing glasses. Both names derive from the four-legged, and therefore 'horselike', base on which they are supported; towel horses, which also stand on four feet, are so called for the same reason.

Cheval mirrors are giant versions of the small toilet mirrors that stand on dressing tables. They are closely similar in design, but intended for full-length viewing. Large mirrors of this type came into vogue in the late eighteenth century after the introduction into England from France in 1773 of a glass-casting technique that made possible the production of large sheets of glass. It was at this date that tall wall-mounted pier glasses, so called because they were mounted on the piers, or columns, between windows, first appeared as a common decorative feature. Despite this important technical advance—previously the glass had been blown into a cylinder, which was slit and the curved sides flattened—it was to be some time before the glass cost less than the even more elaborately carved and gilded frame, such was the expense of manufacturing and transporting it.

Cheval mirrors were dressing mirrors, and had to cater for people of different heights, so they had to be easily adjustable. In most examples, the glass is supported by swivel screws and the feet set on castors. With some, the glass can be raised and lowered like a sash window by means of weights in the uprights.

This mirror was made in about 1845; its rather ponderous interpretation of classical motifs, such as the S scrolls, is characteristic of much early Victorian furniture. The wood is birch, a pale wood resembling the more exotic satinwood of which many eighteenth century cheval mirror frames were made. Birch, which is one of the most beautiful native English woods used in furniture-making, has a close grain and polishes well. It is, however, more usual to find Victorian cheval mirrors made of rosewood or mahogany, which suited the current taste for dark, rich colours.

Cooper-Bridgeman Library   Olivia Jackson Antiques, Westbourne Grove, London W.11

Victorian cheval mirror £45

COMMEMORATIVE WARE The British have commemorated their history on pottery since the first known piece, a delft mug celebrating the coronation of Charles II in 1660. Production, however, was slow until the reigns of George III and George IV, culminating in the reign of Queen Victoria when great events, political struggles, victories and, sometimes, defeats featured on mugs, jugs, plates and bowls.

The flood of commemorative ware, which perhaps reached its highest point in the year of Queen Victoria's Diamond Jubilee in 1897, was accelerated for two reasons. Firstly, by the early nineteenth century there were many more hard and easily worked wares available to the potters and, secondly, the process of transfer-printing had been invented. Both these developments greatly facilitated mass-production and brought about a decrease in the price of commemorative wares.

Roughly concurrent with these technical developments in potting and printing, Britain's communication systems were being drastically revised. This meant that not only were the raw materials becoming available as never before and at increasingly competitive prices, but the fragile, finished articles were able to be transported further afield at ever increasing speed and in ever increasing safety. Commemorative ware also heralded a nation who knew what was happening when it was happening, with the result that it made the

production of commemorative pieces, both for celebratory and for propaganda purposes, infinitely more attractive.

The new railways provided sensational events, taking the place of the earlier Napoleonic victories, and crashes, derailments, bridges and viaducts took over from frigates and lines of battle. Potteries in Sunderland and Stockton-on-Tees produced a large number of 'railway' pieces between 1830 and 1850 and items were still made as late as 1875.

All these pieces were made very cheaply and in large quantities, in total contrast to the earlier style of commemorative ware. The traditions of the original style were maintained in the pieces made as souvenirs of such events as the coronations of William IV and Victoria and the various royal births and marriages. Until the end of the Victorian era, such pieces were generally made of high quality china and produced in relatively small numbers.

The lustre jug shown here is a coronation jug produced to commemorate the marriage of Prince Albert and Queen Victoria on 10th February, 1840. The Queen wore a wedding dress with deep ruffles of Honiton lace at the breast, which is a sure method of identification as to whether the piece is genuinely celebrating the marriage or is just a general piece carrying portraits of the Queen and Prince Consort. A great number of pieces were produced to celebrate this event, but the number of transfers is far more restricted.

A watch-holder.

Admiral Sir James Dundas.

Staffordshire ware and figures range from £7 upwards, depending on condition and rarity of the subject.

STAFFORDSHIRE FIGURES

When Queen Victoria came to the throne in 1837, a new kind of pottery, unlike any which had preceded it, began to appear in that area of north Staffordshire called the 'Potteries'. It rapidly gained in popularity and vast numbers of figures were produced of varying interest and quality.

Made from plaster-of-Paris moulds, the unsophisticated Victorian potters showed great ingenuity in producing an apparently complicated figure from quite simple moulds. As the century progressed, figures gradually stopped being moulded in the round. They developed into flat-back figures intended to be viewed from the front only, usually on a mantelpiece above the fireplace. After 1860 the colours tended to become more subdued and, although many of the figures continued to be brilliantly designed and carefully decorated, much less use was made of the intense cobalt blue of earlier years.

The vast majority of these delightful Staffordshire figures were made in small, primitive factories sometimes employing only a handful of workers, many of whom were children. A bare handful are marked, but most of them carry no factory-mark of any sort. As the figures have grown in popularity, they have also inevitably attracted the attention of the forgers. Some of the output of these forgers is now much better than the early crude attempts at deception. The safeguard, as always, for inexperienced collectors is to find a reliable and specialist dealer.

The watch-holder illustrated here is decorated with the complete range of Staffordshire colours. It illustrates a typically maudling legend in which Llewellyn, Prince of North Wales, slew his favourite hound, Gelert, thinking the dog had attacked his baby son and heir. The child had, in fact, been dragged to safety by Gelert. The blood that Llewellyn had seen was that of the attacking wolf from whom Gelert had rescued the baby.

CHEST OF DRAWERS c.1840

Made of mahogany, this seven-drawer chest-of-drawers bears a close resemblance to the Wellington chest, a tall narrow chest-of-drawers containing about a dozen drawers which can be locked by a single hinged flap, which was introduced c.1815 and named after the Duke. This smaller chest is a less aristocratic and expensive relation of the genuine Wellington, which, because it is both useful and elegant, tends to be sold at surprisingly high prices.

This simple piece bears the original brass swan-neck handles and key-plates, a feature worth noticing on functional period furniture such as this, as it helps the piece maintain its value. Brass for furniture mounts was by this date more widely used than the favoured Georgian metal, bronze.

The original chest-of-drawers first came into general use in the latter part of the late seventeenth century, and was an excellent labour saving device because it facilitated the tidy disposal of household linen and clothes, hitherto stored in inconveniently deep chests with lids. The double chest appeared in the late eighteenth century and soon came to be described as a tallboy or, in American parlance, a highboy.

The small piece of furniture illustrated here is a scaled down version of the original chest-of-drawers, and was probably intended for the storage of smaller items of clothing in a gentleman's dressing room. Given a contemporary use, it would be just as practical for the storage of papers in a study or as a table surface for a lamp and extra storage space in a living-room.

MILITARY CHEST

There is little documentary material on military chests and they are virtually ignored by most furniture experts, possibly because they fall into no specific category and can be regarded equally as luggage or furniture, but this in no way belies their usefulness or significance.

It is thought that they were first designed for the India passage as a convenient method of storage for gentlemen travelling to India to take up a long term of office. They were designed in two sections, the top simply resting on the lower section, and with no protuberances, so that they could be easily encased in a canvas bag for further protection during transit. The handles are always made of brass and inset, the carrying handles at the side lie flat, the corners are mitred in brass and the feet can be readily unscrewed.

Military chests were made up to 1870, often in conjunction with military desks —a desk made in two or three sections on the same principle.

This particular example is made of teak—a heavy, durable wood that neither warps nor shrinks. Chests made of mahogany are frequently found, and they are usually more expensive.

With their decorative brass details, military chests now provide an attractive alternative to the more usual chest of drawers, and the drawings on the left show some typical examples.

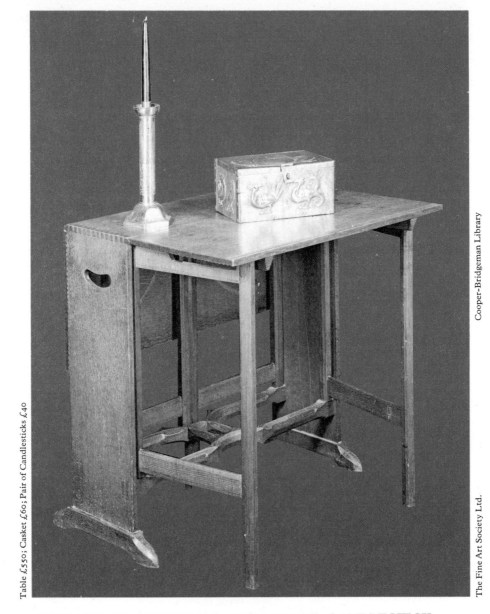

Table £550: Casket £60: Pair of Candlesticks £40

ARTS AND CRAFTS TABLE, CASKET AND CANDLESTICK

There is a clear distinction in Victorian furniture between machine-made and craftsman-made articles. The number of similar objects available obviously affects their value, but in particular the machine-made article lacks evidence of a craftsman's regard for the quality of the wood, for its knots and grain.

In the nineteenth century, there were two conflicting schools of thought on the merits or otherwise of mass production. The Great Exhibition of 1851 was the first serious attempt to show the public that machines were capable of, and indeed excelled at, particular tasks and that it was foolish to expect of them the skills of the craftsman. Sir Henry Cole, who took a large hand in the Exhibition's organization, was calling for better industrial design.

The other school condemned mass production on the grounds of aesthetics. In particular, the Arts and Crafts Movement, which started around 1875 under the inspiration of William Morris, Burne Jones and Rossetti, resulted from a revival of interest in the craftsmanship of previous centuries. The roles of the designer and the craftsman were judged to be equally important in the creation of a work of art.

The objects illustrated here are good examples of this extreme attitude to machine manufacture: that crafts must be practised, from conception to realisation, by machines and not men. Each of these objects was designed and executed by one man: the gate-leg table by Sidney Barnsley, the casket of hammered copper on wood by John Pearson and the hammered brass candlestick by Hugh Wallis.

ARTS AND CRAFTS CHAIRS

The chairs and footstool pictured here were made between 1896 and 1925. Their design and manufacture are associated with the Arts and Crafts Movement, which began gathering momentum in the 1860's. At this time, artists and craftsmen banded together in various groups throughout Britain. Their aim was to help one another to overcome the dreadful uniformity of contemporary machine productions and to reassert the role of the designer-craftsman in an industrial age.

The Movement aimed at simplicity and practicality, coupled with a strong preference for natural materials, forms and colours. In addition, the groups tended to have a mediaeval structure and organization which created an interest in mediaeval techniques and decoration.

In general, the furniture, metalwork and ceramics were inventive and practical adaptations of traditional types with an underlying naivety. The construction and workmanship was absolutely sound. It was an ideal that endured for a long period, partly because many of the groups ran allied colleges of art.

The chair in the centre, with a rush seat and heart-shaped cut-out, is one of four oak chairs by C. F. A. Voysey (1857-1941). Voysey, like many of his associates, turned his hand to many different crafts—architecture and the design of wallpaper, fabrics and furniture.

The high-back chair on the left, with slightly curved, tapered legs is by George Walton (1867-1933). An architect as well as a designer, Walton was closely in touch with Voysey, although the two chairs illustrated here appear to have little in common.

The curiously low chair on the right by an unknown maker has an interlaced leather seat similar to the top of the footstool. It was made in the Russell Workshops Ltd. in Worcestershire.

Set of tiles of the Four Seasons by Minton's: £30 2nd row left and right: £10 each; 3rd row left: £3; right: £5; 4th row left: £3; right: £1 Central panel: £25

Richard Dennis Antiques, 144 Kensington Church Street, W.8 Cooper-Bridgeman Library

VICTORIAN CERAMIC TILES

In the nineteenth century, ceramic tiles were cheap and popular. For purely decorative surfaces, tiles were more widely used than almost any other material and by the last decade of the century they were to be found in most homes.

In 1830 Samuel Wright was granted a patent for the industrial manufacture of ornamental tiles and, in response to rapidly growing demand, many other firms started production in the early years of Victoria's reign. While some Victorian tiles were hand painted or made to a commissioned design, the vast majority were mass-produced by the large industrial potters of the time, the most important of these being Minton's and Maw's. Contemporary catalogues indicate that tiles were generally six inches square, with the exception of floor tiles which were larger. There was a huge variety of designs, but flower motifs were the most popular—often spread over three or four tiles. Many designs reflected the popular interest in Japanese art.

The selection illustrated here is characteristic of the tiles produced by the largest manufacturers of the period; they are of no great commercial value, but still have decorative appeal for the collector. The tiles illustrating the four seasons, made by Minton's, are hand painted and inscribed with the artist's monogram. The four-tile panel with lily design was hand painted by W. B. Simpson & Sons—one of the first firms to exploit the revival of interest in ceramic painting and which turned from general home decoration to specialize in tile painting in 1869. The tiles bearing the knapweed and carnation designs are good examples of the work of the artist-designer William de Morgan, and the blue and white tile depicting Law and Medicine comes from the famous Wedgwood pottery. The tile bearing the design, by an unknown artist, of the wolf and the crane (from one of Aesop's fables) is another Minton product, and the weaver motif on the tile below it is one of a set of twelve trade designs drawn for Minton's by Moyre Smith.

Upper left £45; upper centre £3; upper right £40; lower left £30; lower right over £290

Haslam & Whiteway Ltd., 105 Kensington Church Street and J. & J. May, 40 Kensington Church Street. Cooper-Bridgeman Library

VICTORIAN POTTERY

In the sixty-four years of Queen Victoria's reign, an enormous variety of pottery was produced in England. Technical advances in methods of manufacture, rapidly increasing demand and public interest, spurred on by displays of pottery in the newly-instituted museums, gave rise to a period of creativity and invention. In the early years of the era, moulded jugs and china, often transfer printed in colours, became particularly popular. The moulded jug, illustrated lower left, is a good example of its type. It was made by William Ridgway, Son & Co. of Hanley, Staffordshire, and commemorates the Eglinton Tournament, a Gothic Revival jamboree held in 1839. The type of transfer printing popular in this period is illustrated by the plate, manufactured by W. T. Copeland of Stoke in the 1850's and a souvenir of the popular actor, Albert Smith.

Foreign inspiration is discernible in much of the pottery produced during the Victorian era. The flask-vase (upper left,) decorated with a picture of a crane in the Japanese style, was made by the Watcombe Pottery Co. of South Devon (circa 1875) and is a typical piece of Aesthetic Movement ceramics. The 'Henri Deux' jug (lower right), made with typical Victorian ingenuity and painstaking regard to detail by C. Toft at Minton's, Stoke, is an imitation of the sixteenth-century French pottery now known as 'St. Porchaire'.

As the nineteenth century progressed, there was a reaction against technical elaboration in pottery manufacture; the stoneware produced by Doulton's of Lambeth, for example, was simple and decorated by local art students. The vase, illustrated upper right, was decorated by Louise E. Edwards. The flask-vase, lower centre, in particular represents this progressive trend in Victorian design. Made by the Linthorpe Art pottery at Middlebrough in about 1880 and designed by Christopher Dresser, its geometrical contours and restrained ornamentation presage the fashions in the pottery of the twentieth century.

CELLARET. A cellaret, such as the one illustrated here, is described in the dictionary as a case or receptacle to contain wine. There is a reference to 'a cellar', as a free-standing container for bottles, as early as 1690; the term cellaret, and the article itself, seem to have come into general use after the mid-eighteenth century.

Early Georgian sideboards took the form of side tables, without storage space—hence the need for the cellaret, which was placed under them. The early cellaret was lead-lined and partitioned inside to take bottles; the legs were finished with castors, as in this example.

In the late eighteenth century, sideboards became more elaborate, with fitted drawers, and a cellaret was usually incorporated. It was, however, seldom large enough to hold the variety of drink suited to the habits of an eighteenth century gentleman, and was generally supplemented by a separate cellaret.

The designer Thomas Sheraton classified the cellaret with the wine cistern—a large oval vessel for keeping bottles cool in ice-water, and the sarcophagus, and distinguished it from the bottle-case, which was for square bottles only.

The two wine bottles standing on the cellaret both date from the eighteenth century. Very often, wine bottles of this period bear a name or some other indication of ownership such as a seal, since the buyer of wine normally had it put into his own containers. Bottles were re-used, which obviously limited their production, so they are relatively scarce today. A seal considerably enhances their value. From the early nineteenth century, the use of marks became rare, and with the introduction of ready-bottled wine in the mid-century, the practice gradually died out.

Mahogany cellaret on pillar base c. 1790. £245

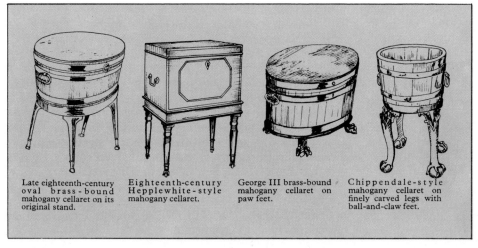

Late eighteenth-century oval brass-bound mahogany cellaret on its original stand.

Eighteenth-century Hepplewhite-style mahogany cellaret.

George III brass-bound mahogany cellaret on paw feet.

Chippendale-style mahogany cellaret on finely carved legs with ball-and-claw feet.

An eighteenth-century
butler's tray with an
oval folding edge.

BUTLER'S TRAY. The tray is an old and simple invention; trays were used in the Middle Ages under the name of 'voyders' (because they were used to 'void' or clear tables). No trays this old survive, and only a few from before 1750.

Trays were much used in the eighteenth century at the dining table and for the elaborate ritual of tea-making. They were often mounted on legs or a folding X-shaped stand and used, in the words of Sheraton, the famous English designer, 'as a sideboard for the butler, who has the care of the liquor at a gentleman's table'. Butler's trays of this type were also used as dumb waiters and for tea. Sheraton also wrote in his *Cabinet Dictionary* of 1803: 'These trays are made of mahogany; half inch Honduras will do for the sides, but the bottoms ought always to be made of Spanish, or other hard wood, otherwise the glasses and slop will leave such a print, on soft wood, as cannot easily be erased'. He gives the measurements as from 27ins. to 30ins. long and 20ins. to 22ins. wide, and says that one end should be made nearly open 'for the convenience of having easy access to the glasses'. Butler's trays of this date often have an ingenious folding edge; the sides and ends of the tray fold down to make a flat table top, generally oval.

Butler's trays were still made in the Victorian and Edwardian period, but seldom have the folding edge, since the making of this demands a high degree of craftsmanship. They are generally made of mahogany and the construction of the X-shaped stand remains much the same; two frames, one slightly smaller than the other, are connected at the top by canvas webbing, and lower down by holes drilled through the centre of the frames and connected by a turned spindle.

COTTAGE PASTILLE BURNERS The craze for cottages in the early nineteenth century can be directly related to the fashion for the simple rustic life. It manifested itself in the form of bonnets, pictures and perhaps most popular of all, pottery and porcelain pastille burners.

These were designed as the direct successor to the more aristocratic cassolette, both being intended for the perfuming of rooms when standards of cleanliness were low and ventilation frequently inadequate.

Before about 1820, pastille burners were mainly made for the homes of the rich but between the years 1820 and 1840, in particular, porcelain and pottery cottages were produced by the thousand, involving such famous names as Rockingham, Coalport, Worcester and the manufacturers of Staffordshire. In fact, not only cottages, but thatched farmhouses, turreted gothic castles, round toll-houses and old-world churches were also made to hold pastilles.

It is often difficult to distinguish the factories at which the burners were made but the following are some of the more obvious indications. Rockingham burners are usually small white cottages of fine porcelain decorated with large coloured flowers. The flowers on the Coalport burners are delicately modelled and profusely scattered over the surface, large sweet-peas, carnations and ranunculus being favoured. Derby cottages are usually large with a lift-off roof and made from a delicate biscuit, similar to that of Wedgwood, who also made small blue cottages encrusted with moss and white flowers.

Early burners are the best buys, later Victorian specimens often being clumsy, crudely modelled and gaudily coloured. The price is affected by the style, size, amount of decoration and the name on the burner.

CHINA FAIRINGS were made in Germany to English designs in the last half of the nineteenth century and provided a cheap and attractive form of souvenir for the Victorian mass market. Made primarily for sale in the numerous English fairgrounds—hence their name—and later in shops, they include groups and figures, match-strikers, pin-holders and watch-holders, the most popular undoubtedly being the humorously captioned groups which are well represented here. These consisted mainly of scenes of courtship and marriage, daily events and topical incidents.

Despite the fact that there are over 230 known different captions, only a handful are now reasonably cheap and available and these usually form the basis of a collection. They include the following:—'The last in bed to put out the light'; '12 months after marriage' and 'Returning at one o'clock in the morning'.

The first mass-produced series of fairings runs from number 2850 to 2899 and the second from 3300 to 3384, although others with four figures outside this series were also made. The figures were first scratched and then impressed on the lower side of the base. It is important to remember that all fairings were of solid, heavy white paste by which they can be distinguished from later poorer quality porcelain imitations.

Thonet rocking chairs cost from about £15 to £40, depending on date and condition.

THONET ROCKING CHAIR

Rockers have been used on cradles since the Middle Ages, but the application of rockers to chairs was not apparently thought of until late in the eighteenth century.

This rocking chair is one of the most graceful designs produced by the Viennese firm of Thonet. The firm was founded by Michael Thonet (1796-1871), a brilliant innovator, businessman and designer of furniture, who invented a series of techniques for bending and shaping wood, mainly beech, using steam, and much of the machinery for applying those techniques to mass production.

His chairs have such universal and timeless appeal that styles thought suitable for a palace in the nineteenth century are still appropriate to a modern interior. They also have the two great advantages of strength and consistent cheapness; Thonet's most popular chair was sold in Austria-Hungary during the 1860s for the same price as three dozen eggs, and for such elegant antiques in the modern idiom, prices are still surprisingly low.

The bentwood process was adopted by other makers but the genuine Thonet products can be identified by the firm's label.

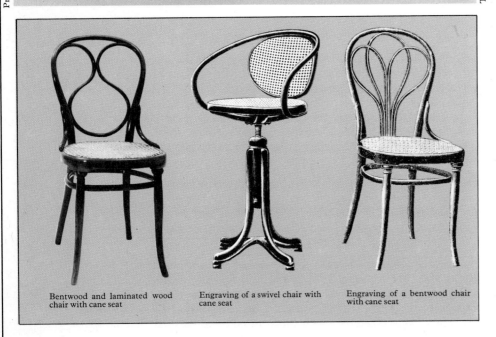

Bentwood and laminated wood chair with cane seat

Engraving of a swivel chair with cane seat

Engraving of a bentwood chair with cane seat

Windsor chair with wheel-back.   Windsor arm chair with comb-back

WINDSOR CHAIR. This illustration shows a Windsor chair with a hoop back made of ash with an elm seat and turned leg and arm supports. With regard to the name, there is a popular story that George III discovered some comfortable stick-back chairs in a cottage at Windsor and ordered some to be made for himself. They were thereafter named Windsor in his honour.

The best Windsor chairs are made of yew and there are two main types: the hoop-back with the spindles socketed into a bow, and the comb-back, which has a top rail shaped like a comb. Both the back spindles and the legs are fixed to the solid wooden seat by dowel joints, a dowel being a headless pin. If there is no evidence of a pin, the joints are probably glued, indicating that the piece has been tampered with or that it is a fairly recent example.

Dresser £98. Willow pattern plates £3.50 each.
Brass jardinière £15.

DRESSER North Wales is the traditional place of origin of this type of solid pine dresser. This one is a genuine antique, probably dating from the late eighteenth century; it has a 'kennel' base, so called because of the central feature in the cupboard section.

Pine furniture is fashionable at the moment. Once it was thought of as coarse and rustic, but a number of lighter, more elegant pieces are now finding their way on to the market. Its light colour looks well with bright colours in a kitchen with modern fittings, for example.

Prices for pine are gradually increasing, but it is still possible to pick up a bargain; under layers of old paint, which can be stripped off with great ease, there is often a very attractive chest of drawers, cupboard or dresser. Working surfaces are usually scrubbed, but a glossier effect is achieved by wax-polishing. The original knobs are wooden but, as here, they have often been replaced with brass handles.

A dresser provides good storage space, but the shelves are often used to great effect for display purposes. Shown here is a collection of blue-and-white willow pattern plates of a type that was very popular in the last century and is still made today by Wedgwood. In the 'kennel' is a brass jardinière.

LARDER CUPBOARD AND STORAGE JARS

This larder, or food cupboard, was made in Ireland in about 1860. The word 'larder' is generally applied to a room, or even a free-standing building such as a game larder, but people who had less space used to keep their food in cupboards like this. The ventilation slats in the doors reveal that it was specially designed for food storage.

The cupboard is made of pine, and like most country-made pine furniture, would in its original state have had turned wooden handles. These, however, are prone to splitting, and here they have been replaced with brass ones of a similar shape. It is rare to find old pine furniture in an absolutely unaltered condition, as the wood does not last long in comparison to hardwoods such as oak. Most pieces older than this have simply rotted away, or become so dilapidated and discoloured that they are of little interest. Fortunately, this cupboard has mellowed to an attractive warm tone.

The stoneware storage jars date from the beginning of this century. Wide-mouthed ones were used for substances such as salt; narrow ones for liquids like vinegar. One of these is a beer flagon. Fitted with new stoppers, such jars can still be useful for storage, as their thick walls preserve the contents by keeping them at an even temperature. They also make an imposing decoration for a kitchen, in view of their very large size.

Vase £40

Peacock dish approximately £350;

Victoria and Albert Museum and Private Collection   Cooper-Bridgeman Library

ART POTTERY

The two pieces illustrated here are characteristic of pottery produced by artist potters in the Arts and Crafts period. Both were inspired by a similar reaction to the technical virtuosity and lack of originality of High Victorian pottery which also stimulated William Morris and his colleagues in other fields.

The earthenware dish, painted with a peacock pattern in 'Persian' colours, was designed by William de Morgan (1839-1917). He was, perhaps, one of the most outstanding of all the artist potters of the late nineteenth century, and he was certainly well known in his lifetime. He began in quite a small way with William Morris and his 'Fine Art Workmen' at Red Lion Square in London. Production consisted mainly of tiles, vases and dishes inspired by Persian pottery. They were often decorated with animals, birds, flowers and fishes in greens, pinks and blues. De Morgan also made some fine dishes with a ruby-red lustre on cream-coloured earthenware.

The earthenware vase, with *sgraffito* decoration through slip, was made in 1888 at C. H. Brannam's Litchdon Pottery at Barnstaple. Brannam's pottery was hand-thrown and called 'Barum ware' after the Roman name for Barnstaple. It was produced from 1879 onwards and, initially, it was of a high quality, but after about 1890—probably due to an insatiable demand—standards dropped. This particular piece is signed with the initials 'W.B.' for William Baron, the decorator, who started his own pottery at Barnstaple in 1899.

VICTORIAN CAMEO GLASS

Cameo glass, a revival of a technique known to the Romans, became one of the most important features of the English glass industry in the latter part of the nineteenth century. Superb examples were produced for exhibitions and the luxury trade.

English cameo work of the late nineteenth century was not really related to contemporary cameo work produced elsewhere. It had figurative decoration and was almost entirely classical in inspiration, unlike the oriental inspiration of the French glassmaker Emile Gallé.

Cameo glass first appeared in England after the Great Exhibition of 1851 and was usually the work of local craftsmen in the Stourbridge area, the centre of nineteenth century English glass making. It is a form of cased or flashed glass which uses several layers of glass in the manufacture of the vessel. Usually it is an opaline glass on a coloured ground with a matt finish, the opaline shape being filled with coloured glass and then marvered. The blank was sent to a decorator's workshop where the outer layer was partially removed and then small steel rods were used to carve the relief. Shadows were obtained by controlling the density of the decoration.

This method of production, requiring such a high degree of craftsmanship, was never a viable commercial proposition. Eventually, with the increased demand for cameo glass, some methods of industrial production were introduced. The glass blank was treated with acid, and an engraving wheel was used. The relief work was done by glass engravers on a considerably thinner base, so that there was less ground to remove for shadowing and commercial pieces could be produced on a larger scale.

The vase decorated with a white flower on orange glass was made by Thomas Webb who managed one of the most famous cameo workshops. The vase designed in an Indian shape with white flowers on a yellow base was made by Joshua Hodgetts, who had been to the Stourbridge School of Art and was a knowledgeable amateur botanist. As illustrated by this vase, he made great use of floral decoration on the wheel-cut commercial work he produced for the firm.

Cameo glass has long been a type of decorative glass requiring great skill and has always been much favoured by collectors.

CHEST OF DRAWERS This is a fine example of a handsome, carefully and solidly built piece of Victorian furniture. The drawers are of mahogany and the front is veneered with burr walnut—wood from the knotty, gnarled area at the base of the tree trunk, which gives the surface a mottled appearance. The maker's name—James Winter & Sons, 101 Wardour Street, Soho, London—is stamped on the left-hand drawer. It is not unusual to find the name of the maker on Victorian pieces, and this is worth looking for on furniture of any distinction.

Although the style of this piece is derived from the classic Georgian design for a chest of drawers, it is in no sense a reproduction; there are many features unknown in eighteenth-century drawer furniture. For example, the graded size of the drawers is in the Georgian tradition, but the plinth joined to the bottom one, and which moves with it, is a later convention. The boldness of the mouldings is also a purely nineteenth-century feature.

Chests of drawers often have interesting handles and knobs, and these form a clear indication of the date of the piece. The plain wooden turned knob of the type shown here was fashionable in the Regency period and again in the 1880s. At other times, folding brass handles would have been more usual.

VICTORIAN CABINET The word 'cabinet' has been applied to a wide variety of furniture. It was first used to describe a writing table or similar piece fitted with lockable drawers and doors to contain documents and valuables; later, it came to mean a type of furniture designed to preserve and display ornaments such as porcelain. Cabinets have always been used for safeguarding and storage. As a result, they are almost always large in scale and elaborate in design, like the one shown here, which is decorated with architectural mouldings and many other features.

This cabinet dates from about 1890 and is stamped 'GILLOWS 16649'. Robert Gillow, a reputable Lancaster joiner to whom the famous designer Hepplewhite was apprenticed in 1761, set up a retail shop in Oxford Street, London, and supplied it with pieces from his Lancaster workshops. The shop flourished during the nineteenth century, and after 1820 every piece of furniture sold there was stamped with the firm's name and individually numbered.

The carcase, or main body, of the cabinet is of oak; it is inlaid with mother of pearl and various lighter-coloured woods. This kind of inlay is known as marquetry, from the French word marqueté, meaning 'speckled' or 'variegated'. Veneers of wood in contrasting colours are cut to fit together into a pattern and glued on to a specially-prepared base. The technique was popular in England in the sixteenth and seventeenth centuries, and was revived by Chippendale and his contemporaries a hundred years later. In the Regency period, it was to a large extent superseded by painted decoration.

Towards the end of the Victorian era, the characteristically heavy furniture of the period was given a lighter look; here, this is achieved by the fine detail of the carving, the pale, spindly inlaid decoration and also by two structural features: the curved glass panels in the sides of the upper section and the contrast between the wide panel at the back of the base and the two thin columns at the front.

Group of stickwork boxes, one barrel-shaped. Prices ranging from £12–£25.

TUNBRIDGE WARE According to existing records, Tunbridge Ware was made as early as the seventeenth century but it was in the nineteenth century that production increased considerably accounting for the majority of Tunbridge ware that we find in the shops today.

Its name, predictably, derives from the town in Kent where the craft was practised. Consisting of a wide variety of objects, Tunbridge ware is characterised by highly decorative wood mosaics. The mosaics rely on the grouping together into bundles of fine sticks, sometimes thinner than a match-stick and between six to ten inches long. These were glued together down the long side in such a way that the pattern, visible at each end, ran the length of each block. Slices were taken from across the block and stuck on to a brown paper backing; they were then veneered on to the box. Although the veneer was only one sixteenth of an inch when sanded down, the use of crude saws led to enormous wastage. These blocks were assembled according to a chart which would list, for example, '2 Holly, 1 Green, 3 Beech'; and the design could be checked against a water-colour pattern on squared paper.

Initially the pieces chosen for this treatment were everyday objects, and

Teapoy, c.1830 possibly by G. and J. Burrows about £40.

these were simply decorated with geometric mosaic patterns, but as the craft developed designs became more sophisticated and the squares, diamonds and star patterns were, in the 1840's, followed by minute mosaic work.

Flowers were a popular early motif and soon afterwards birds and animals. These wares were based on Berlin woolwork of the period.

The teapoy illustrated here is an excellent example of the mosiac inlay in its early phase, when the small geometrical patterns were used. The piece is also decorated with birds and butterflies. and, even more unusual, bees or beetles, marking the first departure from the geometric pattern.

A high point in the history of Tunbridge ware is marked by the large number of makers exhibiting at the Great Exhibition, dominated by the ambitious work of Edmund Nye and his apprentice. Thomas Barton, later his partner and perhaps the greatest manufacturer of all. Amongst their many exhibits was a table made from 129,540 pieces, depicting the grosbeak and the Baltimore oviole.

When buying Tunbridge ware, it is advisable to be aware of Sorrento ware which is still produced in Italy and is similar in appearance, although it lacks its rich coloration and the woods are often, and obviously, dyed. It is also advisable to guard against the poor quality work produced in the 1920's and 30's when there was an attempt to revive the craft.

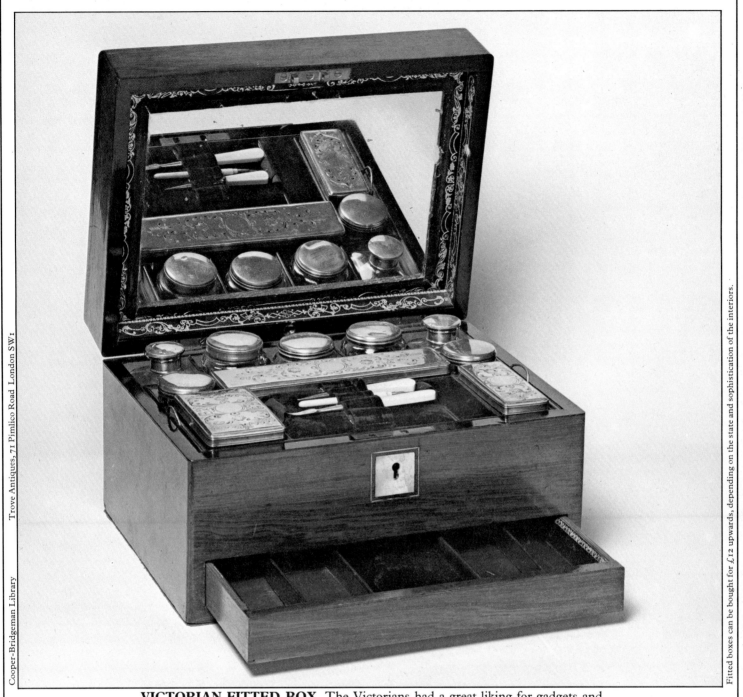

VICTORIAN FITTED BOX. The Victorians had a great liking for gadgets and devices that combined several functions. One of these was the fitted box, which had been used before for holding writing equipment, for example, but which the Victorians brought to a high degree of sophistication.

Fitted boxes were used to hold jewels, cosmetics, medicines, games and sewing, writing, drawing, painting, smoking and picnic equipment—often several of these at once. The box shown here is a dressing-case, and has specially-shaped compartments to hold brushes, combs, bottles, jars, and even manicure equipment. There is a mirror in the lid and a typically ingenious Victorian feature in the base: a secret jewel tray opened by a concealed button.

Many of the boxes that survive are of high quality with elaborate decoration and, as here, solid silver fittings inside. For those who could not afford such luxuries, there were cheaper boxes made mechanically in large numbers. Boxes intended for use while travelling were generally made of hardwood and had fitted leather or cloth outer cases for protection—the Victorians, who had servants, did not care greatly about the weight of their luggage. Boxes for use at home were generally made of silver, lacquer, enamel or papier-mache.

The taste of the time was for heavily-decorated items, and many wooden boxes have elaborate inlay and marquetry work.

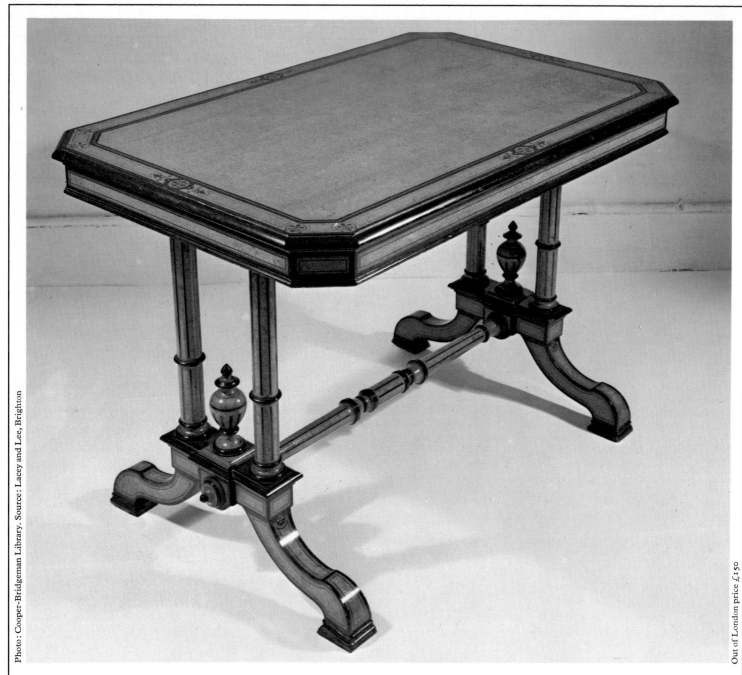

Out of London price £150

LIBRARY TABLE Made of amboyna wood, delicately inlaid with ebony, this table illustrates the fine craftsmanship associated with the best late Victorian furniture—craftsmanship that is very rarely equalled today.

Victorian designers are noted for their imaginative and often astonishing combination of earlier styles and types of decoration in a single piece. Here the designer incorporated some classical motifs, such as the urns on the base, but in a restrained and unostentatious manner. An undoubtedly good piece of furniture, it is surprising that the designer or maker did not follow customary practice by marking or signing it.

Another characteristic of Victorian furniture-makers is that they liked to use unusual woods. Amboyna is pale, with an interesting fleck, and it often gives a piece an attractively light appearance, an often welcome contrast to the traditional 'brown woods' such as mahogany.

Library tables are often indistinguishable from sofa tables, the latter being designed for books rather than writing, and good examples of either are seldom cheap.

VICTORIAN CANTERBURY. Around the end of the eighteenth century, special stands began to be made to hold bound volumes of music. This type of article was known as a 'canterbury', a term explained by Sheraton in his Cabinet Dictionary of 1803: 'The term has of late years been applied to some pieces of cabinet work because, as the story goes, the bishop of that see first gave orders for these pieces. One piece is a small music stand . . . The other piece . . . is a supper-tray, made to stand by a table at supper, with a circular end, and three partitions cross-wise, to hold knives, forks and plates.' A square-ended version of the supper-tray type is shown on the right; it is older than the music stand above and might have been used at a small, intimate supper party. Like its later counter-part, it stands on four turned legs with castors. The music stand has a drawer in the bottom for loose sheets of music.

In early examples of the canterbury, the volumes (or plates) were separated by thin slats or turned spindles, but later ones usually had rows of dowels. In the Regency and early Victorian periods, the design became more and more elaborate, like that of most other pieces of furniture.

Many woods are used for the construction, including mahogany, beech, oak, pine and satinwood veneer on maple. Nowadays, the canterbury is generally used as a magazine rack—a use that ensures a great demand. As a result, they tend to be in short supply, and prices are rather high.

Late eighteenth-century supper-table canterbury with flat top.

GRANDFATHER CLOCK

The famous long-case clock probably originated in England. It is generally known as the 'grandfather' clock, as it was called in a popular song, written by H. C. Work, in 1878.

The need for long-case clocks arose because the heavier weights required for the early eight-day wall clock made it increasingly less safe for hanging on the wall. In about 1660 a tall, wooden, dust-proof case to 'house' the weights and to support the movement and dial was introduced, as well as a detachable glass-fronted hood.

The wooden cases of the early long-case clocks were characterized by narrow trunks which enclosed the weights, while the bob pendulum swung behind the back plate of the movement. After the invention of the anchor escapement, the trunk was widened which also allowed room for the long pendulum. These cases were products of specialist clock-case makers.

In the Victorian period long-case clocks continued to be popular with all classes. Early examples were similar in appearance to those of the late Regency period, except for an over-elaboration of decoration on case and dial. Inlay was also greatly favoured on oak, rosewood and mahogany cases and mouldings became generally heavier. By mid-nineteenth century a local name on the clock dial usually indicated that it had been merely assembled by a stockist of parts.

The example illustrated here was made in about 1850 and has an eight-day striking movement. The case is made of pine, a cheaper wood, which indicates that the clock was probably originally found in a fairly humble household. Later, the pine was either painted white or stained brown, by an owner with social pretensions, to simulate mahogany. The paintwork has now been stripped and the pine is in particularly fine condition because it has been covered and protected for so many years.

The dial is decorated with an enamel painting of 'The Rocket', the first locomotive, invented in 1829. This design is contemporary with the clock, but designs were often added at a later date, transfer-printed, and then painted over. The maker is Richard Cocking of Andover, one of the many provincial clock-makers who produced long-case clocks at this time.

Photo credit: Cooper Bridgeman Library

Source credit: Guildhall Museum Collection

Victorian Watches £300–£500

VICTORIAN WATCHES

The technical skill of the Victorians is seldom seen to better advantage than in the watches which were produced during their era. Apart from seeking to achieve greater reliability in the mechanisms of their watches, the Victorian watch-makers made continual efforts to simplify the initially complex designs. In particular they tried to make their watches more convenient for the user in such details as the methods of winding up the watches and re-setting the hands.

Probably the most important single advance of the nineteenth century was the gradual development and perfection of the detached lever escapement—the heart of the watch—leading to greater precision. Another important area of development was the winding mechanism. Up to the middle of the nineteenth century, watches had generally been wound by separate keys, bulky and inconvenient. Various ingenious keyless winding systems had been invented before the introduction and wide acceptance of a winding button like that used on today's watches.

The fine examples illustrated here are representative of the general high quality of Victorian workmanship. The watch on the left is an experimental 'decimal watch' made by Dover Stratter of Liverpool in 1862. To coincide with its introduction, a pamphlet was published which explained the basis of the decimal time system. The gold and enamel, mid-Victorian watch on the right is by James Ferguson Cole, whose work is now highly prized by collectors. The intricately-patterned eight-day watch in gold, at the bottom, was made by Alexander Watkins in 1851. Its multi-coloured gold dial and engine-turning decoration on dial and case are typical of the designs favoured by some early watch-makers, but which were superseded, soon after this watch was made, by the plain, white enamel dial.

VICTORIAN CAST IRON WASH-STAND It is often difficult to distinguish between Victorian cast iron and steel furniture, although the latter has a more aristocratic lineage. One of the earliest recorded pieces is a chair made of forged steel for the Emperor Rudolf II by Thomas Rucker of Augsburg (1532-1606). It was covered with chiselled reliefs to which were added chiselled steel sculptured figures.

In the Victorian period a number of steel end cast iron bedheads were made as these were durable metals which did not suffer from the disadvantages of wood, such as wood worm. Occasionally matching pieces, such as this wash-stand, were made to go with them but they appear on the market only infrequently and there seems to be every indication that they never became popular.

Seldom made to a really high standard—they were presumably largely designed to meet the pockets of the middle classes—this particular piece is rather exceptional in character and design. Like all cast iron and steel furniture, it has the advantage over wood of a substantial reduction in the thickness of the constructional members which gives it a certain elegance. The ornament consists mainly of steel beads and rosettes, each rivetted individually to the framework. Originally probably painted black, the wash-stand has in recent years been burnished by the sand blasting method and polished. This is frequently carried out because paint seldom withstands the rough treatment of everyday use. Like the majority of Victorian wash-stands, it is marble topped and has a towel rail at either end.

The blue and white ewer and basin, decorated with the traditional willow pattern, are direct descendants of the eighteenth century blue and white porcelain produced by the English in imitation of the Chinese. With very few exceptions, blue and white was made for everyday use, and most factories found it a very good selling line. It was comparatively cheap to produce and helped to finance their more costly and ambitious ventures in polychrome decorated porcelain and figures.

Bed-step commode c. 1840. £60

BED-STEP COMMODE This early Victorian bed-step commode dates from the days when beds, especially four posters, were constructed at such a height from the floor that it was virtually impossible to climb in unaided. Beds generally stood on tall legs and the bedding consisted of a number of mattresses placed one on top of the other, the intention being to prevent the occupant suffering from the severe draughts which were only too apparent in a Victorian house.

Another feature of bedroom practice in the eighteenth and early nineteenth century was the use of a chamber-pot since sanitation, if it existed at all, was usually some distance away and inconvenient. The bed-step generally incorporated a chamber-pot in the upper section, which opened by means of a lid. In this particular example, access to the hollow upper step is by means of a door. The lower step slides out and originally incorporated a wooden surround for the chamber-pot, forming a complete seat.

This example has the characteristic turned legs of the bed-step and is in mahogany, one of the most usual woods, although bed-step commodes were occasionally made in pine or walnut. The treads were originally carpeted but, because of wear, this has been replaced by leather. Although faked library-steps are not unusual, faked bed-steps are virtually unknown.

WORKTABLE.

The earliest worktables were made in the second half of the eighteenth century, a high point in the history of English furniture design, when a number of pieces for specialized purposes were invented.

This example was made in about 1810 to the most up-to-date design. It has a reversible top with a reading stand and backgammon and chess boards, all fashionable features of the time. Leisure and pleasure were serious pursuits that had to be catered for as much by the furniture trade as by any professional entertainer.

Such intricately composed pieces are, of course, expensive. Great care was taken in their making: it required skill to assemble them and fine materials were employed. The exterior is of rosewood; inside, boxwood and ebony are used. The legs are reeded and have paw feet. The workbag, re-covered in velvet is suspended beneath the table, neatly concealing all the paraphernalia of the needlewoman. Though almost certainly intended for the silks and wools of fine needlework, it would be just as suitable for darning materials, and the games boards naturally have the same practical interest today.

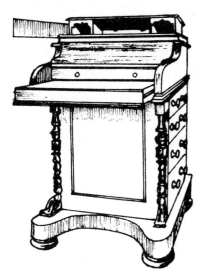

1. Early Victorian burr walnut piano top Davenport with a pull-out adjustable writing slide and cabriole leg supports. £125.

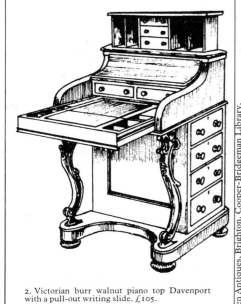

2. Victorian burr walnut piano top Davenport with a pull-out writing slide. £105.

DAVENPORT. A Davenport is a small narrow desk with a writing-slope above and drawers or cupboards below. In the late eighteenth century in the records of the firm of Gillow, the entry 'Captain Davenport—a desk' occurs. This presumably was the origin of the term, although very few examples of early Davenports exist and they only became really popular pieces of furniture in the mid-Victorian period.

They were designed so that the writer could either use the desk in a standing position or, alternatively, seated on a high stool. The sloping top was generally fitted with a brass gallery designed to prevent the writing accessories from slipping, and the drawers usually pulled out from the right hand side, being matched by false drawers on the left, to prevent the user from having to move his knees.

The Davenport was one of the first designs to herald the trend towards compact pieces of furniture including the optimum amount of storage space. As such, it is ideal for the smaller, modern house and a safe buy, since it is too complex a piece of furniture for any but the most ambitious faker to imitate.

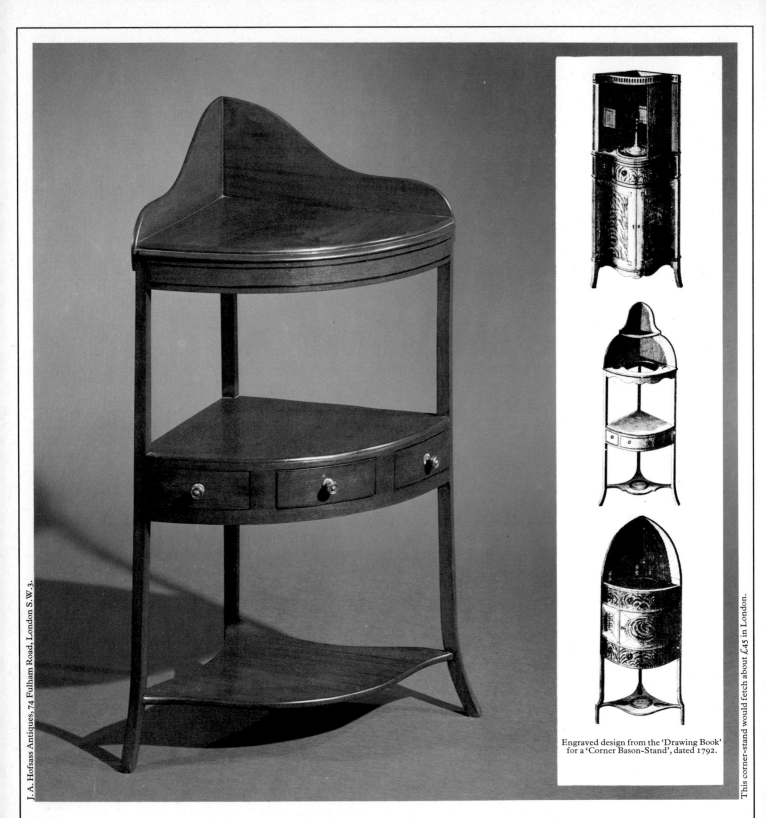

J. A. Hofsass Antiques, 74 Fulham Road, London S.W.3.

Engraved design from the 'Drawing Book'
for a 'Corner Bason-Stand', dated 1792.

This corner-stand would fetch about £45 in London.

This **MAHOGANY CORNER-STAND** with painted ebony banding designed c. 1805 as a wash-stand, has been converted for modern use by the addition of a piece of antique mahogany across the top.

'Bason-stands' were invented in the mid-eighteenth century, and Sheraton designs show that they were often simply excuses for introducing something ornamental to the bedroom or dressing-room, the basins they supported being not much larger than soup plates. When personal hygiene came to be treated more seriously, and design tended to become heavier, the wash-stand became a prominent feature of the Victorian bedroom. The top shelf usually contained a large recess for the basin and ewer and a smaller one for the soap, the original basins often being used nowadays for bulbs and plants. The drawer below was used for toiletries.

WHAT-NOT. This three-tiered walnut what-not has baluster supports and a fretwork gallery. The parian bust and the pair of English vases are of the same period as the what-not. The bowl on the lower shelf is Lowestoft and was made in the eighteenth century.

The term 'what-not' was first coined in the Regency period, presumably as a humorous apology for a more precise description. This useful piece of furniture was designed as a small rectangular stand and was intended for the display of ornaments and curiosities or occasionally to provide shelf and storage space for books and papers.

The Victorian what-not came into general use only in the 1840s, was gradually increased in height and, by the 1850s, was often designed for a corner. It is not to be confused with an *etagère* which was made on a larger scale and often combined with mirror panels and marble.

A Regency period rosewood what-not on turned supports with two drawers to the base, underline the utilitarian purpose of the what-not.

Austin's of Peckham.

c. 1830 The what-not illustrated here would fetch about £40 in a London shop.

Copper £14 – £36; Brass £8.75 – £16

Robin and Valerie Lloyd, Chelsea Antique Market   Cooper-Bridgeman Library

VICTORIAN COPPER AND BRASS Copper was first mined in England at Keswick, Cumberland. This was in the sixteenth century and since that time, it has been used in the manufacture of all types of household wares. Although copper is rust resistant and the impurities are removed by smelting, food cooked in copper vessels acquires an unpleasant flavour. It is for this reason that culinary utensils such as teapots, kettles and saucepans are lined with a thin layer of tin. In 1756 the Society for the Encouragement of Art, Manufactures and Commerce issued a report on the dangers of cooking in copper and brass vessels, remarking: 'Tis therefore presumes, that for the future, none who value the health of their families, will use copper vessels untinned'.

Brass is an alloy of copper and zinc, usually compounded of two parts copper to one part zinc. It is hard, ductile and malleable; it is easily joined, hard wearing and takes a high polish. For this reason, craftsmen chose copper for producing countless candlesticks, chandeliers, fire-irons and fenders, and, in the nineteenth century, bedsteads. Shown here are brass candlesticks, a can originally used for transporting hot water from the fire to the basin or bath, and a three-legged trivet with a porcelain handle, used as a stand for keeping pots and kettles warm by the fire.

The principal place of manufacture was, as it is today, Birmingham. There are sales catalogues still in existence which illustrate the various designs available. The catalogues remained current for so long that it is often difficult to date copper and brass except for candlesticks. Brass examples are the poor man's silver and closely resemble the faster-changing patterns of silver candlesticks.

TEAPOY This rosewood teapoy on a pedestal base, made *c.*1830, differs from earlier versions in so much that it has four feet. The teapoy proper seems to have originated in the East, for the name derives from the Hindu for three (*tin*) and the Persian for foot (*pae*); owing to its associations with tea, it was translated from tinpae to teapoy. The term can be used to describe both the table on which the tea-caddy was kept, and the actual caddy itself mounted on a three-legged pedestal base which was 'used in drawing rooms to prevent the company rising from their seats when taking refreshments.' (George Smith's *Household Furniture* [1808]).

The interior of this teapoy shows four canisters for the various types of tea and the mixing bowls in which the hostess would make her own blend at table. Since tea was notoriously expensive, most teapoys, like caddies and canisters, were fitted with a lock and key.

There is a popular misconception that a teapoy is simply a porcelain tea-canister, but there are no grounds for believing that the word was ever used in this sense. They are only infrequently seen in antique shops and make attractive occasional tables should you be lucky enough to come across one.

VICTORIAN TEA SERVICES Tea and coffee sets formed a major part of the nineteenth century silversmith's output and, as such, are particularly illustrative of the fashions and mixtures of styles of the day. They are also the natural products of an age of great prosperity, when the general rule was one of display and when many considered the ownership of such items to be a necessity rather than a luxury.

From the severe lines of the late eighteenth century styles and the more classical feeling of the subsequent fifteen years, the naturalistic manner evolved. Natural forms, used on silver and plated wares prompted the arrival of gourd-shapes.

The Great Exhibition of 1851 was a turning-point away from the accepted ideas of the previous thirty years. During the period from about 1850 to 1880 the nineteenth century silversmith's facility for artistic variety is seen, perhaps, at its best.

One milk jug illustrated here, made in the workshops of J. B. Hennell of Charlotte Street in 1877, is in the form of a grotesque female figure. It was probably influenced by the political situation of the time and by the growing success of excavators of early remains along the Nile. Made in the Egyptian manner in cast and chased silver and neither harpy nor sphinx, the lady nestles comfortably, arms folded, on three truncated supports.

The silver-gilt milk jug, decorated with insects and butterflies, was made by Mackay, Cunningham and Co. of Edinburgh in 1879, and was inspired by the Japanese exports which began to arrive in Europe during the 1850's. *Japonaiserie* silver was in vogue for about thirty years, reaching its peak of excellence in the 1870's.

BISCUIT TINS The cheapest, most humble objects are often the best records of prevailing fashions and, frequently, the most ingenious. The principal stylistic developments of the nineteenth and twentieth centuries, for instance, can be traced through biscuit tins or the packaging of merchandise.

The supplier who commissioned and used the tins illustrated here was Huntley and Palmer, the biscuit manufacturers of Reading and London. London stagecoaches travelling to and from the West Country frequently stayed at the Crown Hotel opposite the Reading shop of Huntley and Palmer, where biscuits were sold to the passengers. Thomas Huntley's brother, Joseph, was an iron-monger, and he made airtight tins for the biscuits to keep them fresh. At first these tins were laboriously hand made, but by the 1870's tin-printing machines had been invented, making possible the production of tins in a great variety of shape and decoration.

Once the usefulness of the tins was established, other manufacturers quickly followed suit. They were good advertisements for a product and were much admired at the international trade fairs. In 1878 in Paris, Huntley and Palmer won a Grand Prize. The decision of the judges was undoubtedly influenced by the effectiveness of the container's attractive appearance.

The two book and bookshelf tins date from about 1890 and the one in the centre from a little later. The book tin is particularly ingeniously devised and it is hardly surprising that it was a fashionable item at the time of its manufacture.

VICTORIAN SETTEE. A late Victorian furniture style that was still popular well into Edwardian times was a revival of the delicate, supremely elegant, style of the late eighteenth century—the age of Adam, Sheraton and Hepplewhite.

The settee, which is basically a double or triple chair—and therefore often made as part of a set including chairs—resembling, in its earliest form, two wing-back chairs of the Restoration period—is an essentially formal piece and a popular Georgian type of seat furniture. Even in this example, where the back and sides are upholstered (the sides are, incidentally, removable), the back is too upright for comfort and the wooden arm-rests are too hard. It contrasts with the stuffed sofa, which acquired its comfortable spiral springs in the nineteenth century; it was designed specifically for relaxation and corresponds to the raised platform covered in carpets and cushions favoured in Eastern countries.

Satinwood, here delicately painted with wreaths and cameos in a light-hearted neo-classical style, was used extensively as a veneer in the eighteenth century: the pale colouring and fine grain were much admired. Only in the succeeding century was it used as a solid wood for chairs, and particularly for painted furniture in the late Georgian manner. It was an imported wood from the East and West Indies.

Phelps Ltd, 129-135 St Margaret's Road, Twickenham Cooper-Bridgeman Library

VICTORIAN HALL FURNITURE Hall chairs, generally found in pairs, were designed to provide a temporary seat in a hall or passage for servants or for visitors waiting to be announced. Since they were not meant to be sat on for any length of time, there was seldom any attempt to make them comfortable. A typical hall chair is made of mahogany with a flat wooden seat without any upholstery or caning. The back is generally carved.

When this type of chair was first made in the early eighteenth century, the owner's coat of arms would have been painted on a shield on the back. The right-hand chair in the picture, although Victorian, is very like the early type, and has a shield set in a roundel on the back. There is no sign, however, that it was ever painted.

The left-hand chair is a more typically Victorian piece, with characteristically heavy carving disguising the 'vase' shape of the back. Both chairs, however, have the same kind of seats and turned legs.

The brass umbrella stand is of a traditional design with a tubular frame, a grid at the top to keep umbrellas and sticks upright, and a tray at the bottom to catch drips—a vital feature in the days before the invention of washable floor coverings and efficient carpet cleaning. It is quite a plain piece; many Victorian umbrella stands are elaborate constructions incorporating stags' antlers, elephants' feet and even stranger objects.

VICTORIAN WORCESTER PORCELAIN

In the eighteenth century, English porcelain had been produced mainly for the home market and, while making articles of a high quality, the English manufacturers couldn't compete with the leading producers on the continent. In the Victorian era the position was reversed; the quality of English porcelain improved considerably and continental designers, artists and modellers crossed the Channel in large numbers to find work in England.

In 1837, at the beginning of the Victorian period, Worcester was the home of many important porcelain manufacturers, the most famous being Graingers, Chamberlains and the firm of Flight, Barr and Barr. These firms were generally small and new partnerships were periodically formed and re-formed. In particular, Flight, Barr and Barr joined Chamberlains in 1840 to form the new firm of Chamberlain & Co., which in turn was succeeded in 1852 by the partnership of Kerr and Binns.

After a very successful period, Kerr and Binns gave way to the famous Royal Worcester Porcelain Company, established in 1862 under R. W. Binns. Some of their glazed figures and groups rival the best eighteenth century classics and the charming series of boys and girls in prim Kate Greenaway style dress occur in an enormous variety of objects such as candlesticks, centrepieces for the table, fruit baskets, menu holders, candle snuffers or simple ornaments. The artist and modeller responsible for these and other Royal Worcester designs, in particular the nautilus shell vases illustrated here, was James Hadley who left the firm in 1896 to establish his own rival factory in Worcester. The output of the Royal Worcester Company represents the best of Worcester porcelain: it is varied and always of high quality.

proost Turnhout (Belgium)

PRINTED IN BELGIUM